THE
ROYAL
FAMILY

THE
ROYAL
FAMILY

Edited by
Duncan Hill • Alison Gauntlett • Sarah Rickayzen • Gareth Thomas

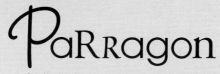

Bath · New York · Singapore · Hong Kong · Cologne · Delhi · Melbourne

First published by Parragon in 2007

Parragon
Queen Street House, 4 Queen Street, Bath, BA1 1HE, UK

Produced by Atlantic Publishing

Photographs © Associated Newspapers Archive
Text © Parragon Books Ltd 2007

ISBN 978-1-4054-8808-2
Printed in China

Contents

The House of Windsor

Ninety years ago the House of Windsor was born amidst the turmoil of the First World War. George V, mindful of the Royal Family's links with the German monarchy (through his grandmother's marriage to Prince Albert) and the negative feelings this could engender, changed the dynastic name from Saxe-Coburg-Gotha to Windsor.

Since then, the Royal House has reigned through a period of unprecedented political and social change; the families of 1918, welcoming their war-weary men home from the horrors of the Front, could not have imagined the Britain of today with its advances in medicine, technology, public health and housing, education, mass communications, political and social attitudes. Then, as the Great War was drawing to a close, Britain still stood at the center of its Empire, and indeed the world; with a Royal Family, distant yet deeply revered by its people. Today, in the first decade of the 21st century, the Empire has long since vanished, and the media and public scrutiny of the Royals has seen an end to the unquestioning loyalties of the past.

The story of the Windsors, especially through the early part of their reign, is a fascinating, and at times, dramatic one: George V 's death in 1936 led to a constitutional crisis at the end of the year when his eldest son and heir, Edward VIII abdicated the crown in order to marry Wallis Simpson, an American divorcée. Prince Albert, his second son, was a reluctant king: his shy personality and, at times, severe stammer did not mark him out as a natural monarch; but with the support of his wife and the backing of the country, he took the responsibility and the title of King George VI and restored public confidence in the Royal Family. During the Second World War, their children, the young Princesses Elizabeth and Margaret, were evacuated to the country, but the King and Queen remained at Buckingham Palace or nearby Windsor even during the Blitz, making many morale-boosting visits to the ordinary people of London and the rest of the country.

Sadly, the War took its toll on the King's health; he was also a heavy smoker and lung cancer caused an

early death at the age of 56 in 1952. His eldest daughter, known as a child as "Lillibet" by the family, heard of her father's death whilst on a tour of Kenya. Having left Britain as a princess, she returned as its Queen and has led the country as its monarch for the past 55 years.

These years have not been without their trials and tribulations—the very public separation and divorce of the Prince and Princess of Wales followed by the devastating fire at Windsor Castle led the Queen to describe 1992 as her "annus horribilis"; in 1997 Diana's death in a car crash in Paris brought more grief and sorrow to the Royals, not least the young Princes, William and Harry. These events have, however, been counterbalanced by much happier ones: the Queen and the Duke of Edinburgh's silver and golden wedding anniversaries; the Queen's Silver Jubilee; and in 2002, the Golden Jubilee, celebrating 50 years since her accession to the throne.

As Head of State, Queen Elizabeth II has a vital and visible role to play in the life of the nation: an extensive schedule of visits by her and other members of the Royal Family; meeting the public and supporting businesses, charities, and public bodies ensures links with her people are maintained and strengthened.

Internationally, her role as Head of the Commonwealth and visits to all parts of the world help to foster and promote positive international relations. Modern communications and "instant" news has meant that many of the members of the Royal Family are recognized the world over; inevitably this has led to increased media interest—some may even say intrusion—and a fascination for all things Royal. Being in the public gaze, almost on a daily basis, is something the House of Windsor has had to adapt to, and to accept that they will not always be portrayed in the best of lights. Nevertheless, the Queen and her family are still regarded with great affection and national pride; providing a focus that fosters stability and continuity for the nation.

This book brings together more than 700 photographs from the archives of the *Daily Mail*. Many of them date back to the early years of the 20th century—pictures of George V on the battlefields during the Great War, the young Elizabeth, the Duchess of York on her wedding day—and provide a fascinating, and at times, intimate glimpse of a bygone age. These historic and beautiful pictures are combined, for the first time, with more recent photographs; together, these stunning images catalog the life of the remarkable House of Windsor.

The Young Royals

Edward and Albert were the eldest of six children born to George V and Queen Mary. As the first-born, Edward was the natural heir to the throne.

Below right: Edward shooting at Balmoral in 1911. Meanwhile, his father was hunting tigers while on a state visit to India.

Opposite right: Edward, resplendent in naval uniform at Buckingham Palace in 1911, shortly after his father's Coronation as King George V, and his own investiture as the Prince of Wales.

Opposite above left: Even as a young man the Prince was renowned for his attention to detail when it came to being properly dressed for any given occasion.

Below: A somewhat awkward and unacademic youth, Edward's younger brother, Prince Albert led a rather unhappy childhood, no doubt partly on account of the social stigma associated with his left-handedness. However, he would later excel at sports, particularly tennis, although here he can be seen playing golf.

Above right: Prince Albert, the Duke of York, during his naval schooling, aged 16.

Center right: The Prince of Wales and his younger sister, Princess Mary, playing with Caesar, the late King Edward's favorite dog, at Frogmore.

Opposite below left: Prince John, the youngest of George V and Queen Mary's six children suffered from epilepsy. He spent his life hidden from public view and died an early death in 1919.

The Great War

Opposite below left: World War I broke out in 1914 and the King set to work rallying the troops. He visited the trenches on five occasions to conduct inspections and present medals for bravery.

Opposite below right: King George met with General Congreve and Sir Henry Rawlinson on a visit to the Western Front. The King was no stranger to uniform; he had enjoyed a career in the Royal Navy and had risen to the rank of commander.

Below: Britain and France were allied during the conflict and here the King and Queen are pictured with their French counterparts, President and Madame Poincaré.

Left: The King also took the time to visit French villagers whose lives were seriously disrupted by the fighting.

Opposite above: The teenage Princes, Edward and Albert, with their sister, Mary, at Balmoral just before the outbreak of war. Prince Albert saw action during the conflict at the great naval battle of Jutland.

Beginning Royal Duties

Right: After the war, the Princes began to assume royal duties on behalf of the King. Here Prince Albert, who had become the Duke of York, is pictured kicking-off a charity soccer game between Tottenham Hotspur and Corinthians at White Hart Lane.

Opposite below left: The Prince showed continued support for sport by touring Cambridge Boat House in March 1920.

Opposite below right: Meanwhile, his brother, the Prince of Wales, demonstrated a commitment to academia when he was installed as the Chancellor of the University of Wales in 1921.

Below: The Duke participated in a shooting party with Lord Pembroke in October 1920. Here the two men are pictured examining their "bag."

Opposite above: The Duke's activities were not limited to sporting life. Here he is pictured giving his support to the post-war rejuvenation of the nation by attending the Reparations for the Empire exhibit at Wembley.

The Duke's Engagement

Above: Elizabeth Bowes-Lyon, the daughter of the Earl and Countess of Strathmore had caught Prince Albert's attention when they had met as children. He was immediately attracted to her ease with people, strength of character, and commitment to duty.

Opposite: Initially, Elizabeth is thought to have been reluctant to marry into the Royal Family, but Albert was so in love with her that he persevered and the couple were finally engaged in January 1923.

Right: Elizabeth and Albert posed for a series of photographs to mark the occasion of their engagement on January 14, 1923. Here they are pictured in a relaxed manner.

The Royal Wedding

Opposite above: Albert and Elizabeth were married just three months after their engagement. Elizabeth is pictured leaving her London home on the way to the ceremony.

Above: The King and Queen on their way to the wedding. They were very pleased with their son's choice of bride. They found Elizabeth to be a charming "breath of fresh air."

Opposite below: The wedding took place at Westminster Abbey on April 26, 1923.

Left: The happy couple are captured after their wedding, on their way to the station to start their honeymoon.

The Honeymoon

Above: The couple took their honeymoon at Polesden Lacey in Surrey. Here they are seen relaxing after a game of golf.

Opposite: The Duke and Duchess of York take a walk through the grounds of Polesden Lacey. Once the honeymoon was over, they spent the first few years of their marriage living in Bruton Street, London.

Left: Upon marrying Albert, Elizabeth became the Duchess of York. Here the Duke and Duchess are pictured with Queen Mary at Balmoral in 1924.

The British Empire Exhibition

Opposite above: In April 1924, the King opened the British Empire Exhibition at Wembley to bolster economic and cultural ties within the Empire. The King returned in May with the Royal Family to attend the Empire Thanksgiving Service.

Opposite below: The Royal Family visited the exhibition on several occasions, here Queen Mary arrives with her son, Prince George.

Left: The Duchess of York attends a garden party for the "Lest We Forget" Association in East Molesey in July 1924.

Above: Later in the year, the Duke and Duchess of York visited the Millwall Docks to talk with workers. After World War I Albert became President of the Industrial Welfare Society, and was actively involved in establishing programs to help young workers.

The King in France

Above: King George V paid tribute at the the Tomb of the Unknown Soldier at the Arc de Triomphe in Paris in 1925. He left a wreath bearing the inscription "From George V, to the unknown soldier."

Right: The King and Queen in the Great Hall of Bristol University, where they opened new buildings in June 1925.

Opposite above right: The King and Queen pictured with the War Minister, Stephen Walsh. Walsh was a member of the Labour Government, which had been elected in 1924 for the first time ever.

Opposite above left: The Duke of York took part in the celebrations for the centenary of Norwich Museum in October 1925.

Opposite below: The Duke of York with dignitaries, including the Vice-Chancellor, the Chief Constable, the Pro Vice-Chancellor, and the Lord Mayor, whilst on a visit to Leeds in 1925. Despite numerous public appearances, the Duke often struggled with public speaking on account of a severe stammer.

The Duchess at the Circus

Left: Elizabeth took delight in a trip to the circus at Wembley with the Archbishop of Canterbury and the Lord Mayor of London.

Opposite: The Duke of York with his father, the King, at Balmoral, having welcomed King Boris of Bulgaria for a brief visit.

Above: The King and Queen enjoyed a day at the races. Here they are pictured on their way to Ascot.

Playing Tennis at Wimbledon

Opposite right: The Duke of York was a keen sportsman and a good tennis player. Here he is seen playing in the Men's Doubles Championship at Wimbledon in 1926. He was the first member of the Royal Family to participate in the tournament.

Opposite left above: The Duke was partnered by Sir Louis Grieg, the chairman of the All England Lawn Tennis Club.

Opposite left below: The Duchess of York was a happy spectator, when watching her husband compete in the Championship.

Below: As well as tennis, the Duke also enjoyed shooting; here he is pictured taking part in a shooting party at Salphay Woods near Ripon in November 1926.

Left: The Duchess of York spent a day watching the horseracing at Cheltenham.

The Birth of Princess Elizabeth

Opposite: Princess Elizabeth was born on April 21, 1926. The Duke and Duchess were presented with a teddy bear by a well-wisher on a trip to the movies shortly after the birth.

Right: Elizabeth on a drive from Buckingham Palace in 1927, accompanied by her nanny, Clare "Allah" Knight.

Below left: The following year, the young Princess Elizabeth, aged two, leaving her Piccadilly home for a drive with her nanny.

Below right: A photograph of Elizabeth in the grounds of Windsor Castle in 1927.

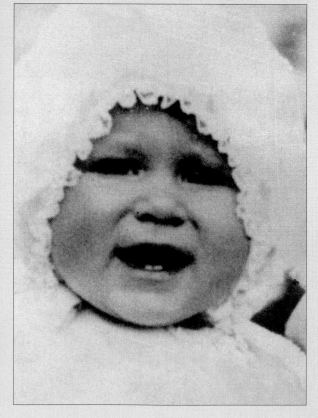

A Visit to Australia

Below: From January to June 1927 the Duke and Duchess of York embarked on a tour of Australia and New Zealand. On the long journey, the Duke passed some time by playing tennis quoits on the deck of the ship, the H.M.S. *Renown*, here watched by his wife.

Opposite below left: The Duchess was not simply a spectator, she also participated in the game, playing here alongside her husband.

Opposite below right: While in New Zealand, the Duchess of York went fishing for trout at Tokaanu, Lake Wanaka, on the South Island in June 1927.

Right: The Duke being lathered and shaved in preparation for his "ducking" en route to Australia. "Ducking" was part of a naval tradition for any seaman who had not previously crossed the equator.

Opposite above: A procession of automobiles carried the Duke and Duchess to Sydney Town Hall for the public reception of the Royal tourists. Their arrival in the city attracted a crowd of over one million people.

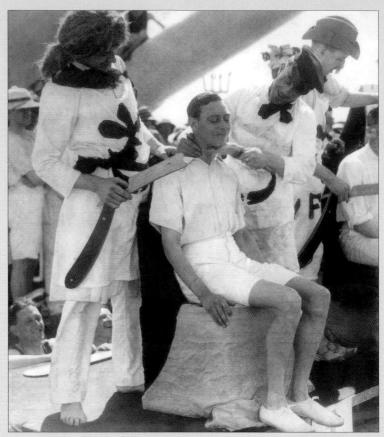

Freedom of the City

Left: After returning from their Antipodean tour, the Duke and Duchess visited University College. They made sure to travel via the newly reconstructed Quadrant in Regent Street, where crowds thronged the sidewalks to cheer them.

Opposite above: The Duke takes part in the celebrations in Glasgow, where the Duchess was given the Freedom of the City in September 1927.

Opposite below: In October, the Duke took part in the Quorn Hunt at Wymeswold, Leicestershire with the socialite the Maharanee of Cooch Behar.

Below: The following February, the Duke and Duchess attended the Salvation Army Composers' Festival at the Congress Hall, Linscott Road, Clapton.

A Busy Schedule

Below: The Duke and Duchess of York were in attendance at the Braemar Games in September 1929.

Opposite above right: The Duke of York is pictured in his kilt after leaving a sitting of the Assembly of the Church of Scotland in Edinburgh in October 1929.

Opposite left: The Duke and Duchess of York are snapped leaving a function in Bethnal Green in November 1929.

Left: The Duke of York conducted an inspection of the training ship *Mercury* at Hamble just before Christmas 1929.

Opposite right below: The Duke, appropriately attired, inspected the Queen's Own Cameron Highlanders during a visit to Fort William the following year.

Promoting Health and Education

Below right: The Duchess of York was introduced to a new-born baby when she opened a new wing at the North Hertfordshire and South Bedfordshire Hospital in Hitchin in July 1929.

Right: The Duke of York declared the opening of new sports fields at Hampton Wick, London in May 1930.

Opposite above: The Duke and Duchess walked along Britannia Pier in April 1931, whilst on a visit to Yarmouth to support the annual conference of the National Union of Teachers taking place in the town.

Opposite below: The following month, the Duchess chatted with nurses when she opened an extension of Harrow and Wealdstone Hospital.

Below left: The Duke pictured on the train traveling to Wembley to address ten thousand children from elementary schools across London.

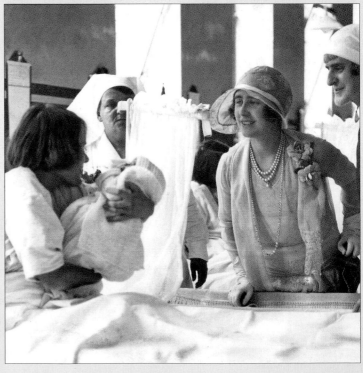

A Visit to Paris

Right: In 1931, the Duke and Duchess of York took a trip to Paris. Here they are pictured leaving the Elysée Palace following a luncheon with the French President.

Above: The Duke and Duchess also visited the Town Hall of the city of Paris where a civic reception was held in their honor. They were photographed with the President of the Municipal Council and the British Ambassador.

Opposite above: The following year the Duke and Duchess were in Liverpool, where they paid a fleeting visit to the city's cathedral.

Opposite below: In March 1932, they visited Cardiff, where the people of Wales presented the couple with a miniature house (which can be seen on the right) for the young Princess Elizabeth to play with.

Southampton

Below: In July 1932 the Duke and Duchess of York attended the Royal Show in Southampton. Here Elizabeth is being introduced to members of the council.

Right: The Royal couple also opened a new civic center, where a group of Girl Guides and Boy Scouts had formed a guard of honor.

Opposite above: The Duchess returned to the city in 1933 with the King and Queen to open the world's largest dry dock.

Opposite below: The Duchess of York and Queen Mary were also seen together at the Royal Opera House in June 1933. This time they were accompanied by the Duke of York.

The Young Princesses

Opposite left: On August 21, 1930 Elizabeth gave birth to her second daughter, Margaret Rose. Here the young Elizabeth and Margaret pose for a photograph at the home of their grandparents, the Earl and Countess of Strathmore.

Opposite below right: The Duchess of York attended the Abergeldie Castle Fête in 1933, with her two daughters, Princess Elizabeth, aged seven, and Princess Margaret Rose, aged three. A picture of Buckingham Palace is visible on the Duchess's purse.

Opposite above right: The young Princess Elizabeth chats to the Countess of Airlie.

Left: In January 1934 Princess Elizabeth accompanied her mother on a trip to the circus at Olympia.

Above: The Duchess of York is pictured with her two young daughters in 1934.

The Princesses Begin Their Duties

Opposite below left: The young princesses became involved in formal functions at a young age. Here they attended a tree-planting ceremony at Windsor Great Park.

Left: The Duchess of York took her two daughters to meet soldiers who had suffered permanent injuries during World War I.

Opposite above: The Queen, the Princess Royal, and the Duchess of York, with Princess Elizabeth on their way down The Mall to watch the Trooping the Color parade at Horse Guards Parade.

Opposite below right: Princess Elizabeth leaving Westminster Abbey with her grandparents, King George and Queen Mary.

Below: The Princesses Elizabeth and Margaret, with their parents, meeting members of the Royal Company of Archers.

Working the Land

Opposite right: The Duchess of York helped to dig a potato plot at the vegetable gardens of the Sheffield unemployed during a visit to inspect the mines in July 1934.

Opposite left: Three months earlier the Duke was pictured playing golf in the rain at Roehampton. To avoid getting wet he put waterproof pants on over his clothes.

Below: After an illness, the Duke was unable to make a visit to the annual boys' camp he ran at Southwold in Suffolk. Instead he addressed the boys and their supervisors at Buckingham Palace before they set off.

Right: The Duke was able to attend the next camp. He watched and also participated in many of the sports at the camp and is seen here playing soccer.

The Duke of Kent's Wedding

Above: In 1934, the King's fourth son, Prince George, became Duke of Kent. In the same year he married Princess Marina of Greece. This photograph was taken when the Duke took his fiancée and her parents to meet his own parents at Balmoral.

Right: Once married, the new Duchess of Kent began her royal duties. Here she is pictured with her husband and the Duke and Duchess of York leaving St. Paul's Cathedral, after the King George V Silver Jubilee Celebration Service, the year after their wedding.

Opposite above: The Duke and Duchess of York boarding an airliner at Hendon as they prepared to visit the International Exhibition in Brussels. Whilst this was to be the Duchess's first flight, the Duke had previously become the first Royal to obtain a pilot's license.

Opposite below: In May 1934 the Duke of York attended the British Legion Service and inspected the standards on Horse Guards Parade.

King George's Silver Jubilee

Below left: King George greeting one of his admirals aboard the Royal Yacht in 1935, the year of the Silver Jubilee celebrations which commemorated the 25th anniversary of his accession to the throne.

Right: Crowds lined the Victoria Embankment, London, to catch a glimpse of the King and Queen as they returned from the Jubilee celebration service at St. Paul's.

Below right: During the Temple Bar Ceremony the Lord Mayor of London presented the King with the ceremonial sword that is the symbol of the City of London's independence.

Opposite: The official Jubilee Portrait of the King and Queen, commissioned to mark the occasion of his twenty-five years as King.

George V's 70th Birthday

Below: Wearing the uniform of the Irish Guards, the King took part in the Trooping the Color ceremony at Horse Guards Parade, on the occasion of his 70th birthday in June 1935.

Opposite above: Prince Edward, the first son of the Duke and Duchess of Kent, was born in October 1935.

Right: A month after his son's birth, the Duke of Kent accompanied his brother, the Duke of York, on Remembrance Day at the Cenotaph.

Opposite below: Princess Elizabeth with the corgi dog, Dookie and Princess Margaret with the corgi dog, Janie at the Royal Lodge at Windsor the following year.

The Death of King George V

Left: King George V died on January 20, 1936 at Sandringham House. His body was taken by train to London for the funeral, where the coffin is pictured being carried from the carriage at King's Cross station.

Opposite below: The coffin was taken from King's Cross to the Great Hall at the Palace of Westminster for the funeral.

Opposite above: The King's body lying-in-state in Westminster Hall. Prior to the funeral, long lines of people filed passed the bier to pay their last respects.

Above: Long lines also formed at Windsor Castle, where wreaths and flowers covered the lawn on the south side of the chapel and rested along the length of the wall on the north side.

King Edward VIII

Opposite: The closing hours of the lying-in-state of George V before the funeral on January 28.

Below: The day after the King's death, the Prince of Wales was proclaimed King Edward VIII. Here he is pictured with his brothers, the Duke of Kent, the Duke of York, and the Duke of Gloucester, at the time of his accession to the throne.

Left: King Edward VIII delivered his first radio broadcast to his subjects from Broadcasting House in March 1936.

The Abdication Crisis

Opposite above left: Within months of Edward's accession to the throne, scandal erupted when the King's relationship with a married woman (Mrs. Wallis Simpson) became common knowledge, and pressure mounted for him to abdicate.

Opposite above right: In December Edward relented and made his abdication speech from Windsor Castle.

Opposite below: The King left the country to be with Wallis in France, where they married just six months later.

Right: Edward and Wallis Simpson on their wedding day.

Below: After abdicating the throne, Edward became the Duke of Windsor and as his wife, Wallis became the Duchess. They are pictured at the Chateau de Cande, France, where they had been married. The pair made their home in France and spent much of their time there until his death in 1972 and hers in 1986.

The Coronation of George VI

Opposite below: After Edward abdicated, his brother, Prince Albert acceded the throne and became King George VI. His Coronation took place on May 12, 1937. Here the King and the Queen are pictured leaving for the Abbey in the state coach.

Opposite above: After traveling down The Mall, the King's carriage passed under Admiralty Arch.

Right: The King was closely followed by his brothers, the Dukes of Gloucester and Kent, riding on horseback.

Below right: A long procession followed the King's coach. The next to pass through Admiralty Arch were the Yeoman of the Guard, or Beefeaters. They were followed by the Watermen.

Below left: After passing under the Arch, the procession pressed on toward Westminster Abbey, here it is pictured on Northumberland Avenue.

At the Abbey

Previous page: Once in the Abbey, the King swore an oath and received communion.

Opposite: King Edward's Chair, where the act of Coronation would take place, sat in the foreground while the King made his oath and communion. George VI joined a tradition, dating back more than six hundred years, when he was crowned on the medieval throne.

Above: Queen Mary, preceded by the Princesses, walks through the Choir toward the west door of the Abbey after the Coronation.

Left: The new King and the Royal Family celebrate the Coronation with the crowds from the balcony of Buckingham Palace.

Popular Support

Bottom: People celebrated the Coronation across the country. Some even slept outside Buckingham Palace to ensure themselves a prime position to view the celebrations the next day.

Right: Many of those who did not camp out overnight for the best positions used periscopes to get a glimpse of the procession.

Opposite below: Street parties were held across the country during Coronation week. This picture shows a children's party in Old Pye Street.

Opposite above right: Streets were also decorated for the occasion. In this picture Vine Street in Clerkenwell is awash with flags.

Opposite above left: Cheering crowds thronged Piccadilly Circus to show their support.

Below: Parties were not just held in the streets, these people celebrated the Coronation at a cabaret show in the Mayfair Hotel.

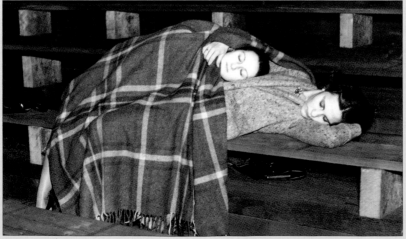

Taking to the New Job

Opposite above: After the euphoria of the Coronation and the turbulence of the abdication crisis, the new King and Queen began to restore a sense of normality to the monarchy. In March 1938 the King and Queen toured a series of housing projects in London. Here they are pictured chatting to a woman with laundry on the line at Armoury House, Wandsworth Plain.

Opposite below: Two months later, the King inspected and presented colors to the Grenadier Guards.

Below left: The Queen and the Princesses, dressed in kilts, attended a bazaar at Crathie Church in September 1938.

Right: The King affectionately inspects his daughters, dressed in their Girl Guides outfits. One thousand Girl Guides had been invited to Windsor Castle and the occasion marked the first official appearance of either princess in uniform.

Below right: The Queen and her daughters reviewed the Christmas displays on a tour of the toy departments of London's big stores.

Supporting the Sports and the Arts

Left: The King and Queen entertained the French President LeBrun and his wife at the Royal Opera House in Covent Garden in March 1939. Here the Queen hands her fur wrap to an officer as she arrives.

Opposite above: President and Madame LeBrun, the King and Queen, Queen Mary and other members of the Royal Family stand for the playing of the French and British anthems before the gala performance by the Vic-Wells Ballet.

Below: The King presented the Football Association Cup to Jimmie Guthrie of Portsmouth FC following his team's 4-1 victory over Wolverhampton Wanderers in the final. The following season the war interrupted the tournament and the final was not be played again until 1946.

Opposite below: Princess Elizabeth accompanied her parents to the All-Star Coliseum Show in 1939.

Trip to Canada

Opposite: The King and Queen leave the Palace to begin their trip to Canada in May 1939.

Left: Standing on deck during their outbound voyage to Canada.

Below: The King and Queen tried to see as much of Canada as possible and traveled from coast to coast. Here they are pictured in the Rocky Mountains, on the lower slopes of Mount Robson, where the villagers collected to cheer them.

In the USA

Opposite: Whilst visiting Canada, the Royal Party took a detour to the United States in June 1939. Here their cavalcade passes the Capitol Building taking the King and Queen to meet President Roosevelt at the White House.

Above: The Royal Family's transport back from North America heads toward Southampton with an escort from the Royal Air Force.

Left: The return of the King and Queen is celebrated as they move through the streets with the Princesses.

The King Prepares for War

Right: Just over twenty years after peace was agreed between Britain and Germany, the two nations once again found themselves at war. The King and Queen are pictured on September 3, 1939 following his broadcast to the nation announcing the outbreak of war.

Opposite below: The King expressed an interest in London's air defenses when he inspected a model barrage balloon in October 1939.

Below: In order to remain informed of the latest military technology, the King tried out a Bren gun during an inspection of a small arms factory in June 1940.

Opposite above: The King also had responsibilities for the Canadian Army. Here he is pictured with Major General Andrew McNaughton, the head of his Canadian forces, in April 1940.

Braving the Blitz

Above: King George VI inspected bomb damage in Bristol during mid-December 1940. Earlier in the month the city had been hit by two major attacks.

Opposite above: The King met nurses from the Bristol Children's Hospital which had been hit during an air raid.

Right: The King and the Queen toured the damage in Salford, Lancashire.

Opposite below: Amid the debris from a bombed London hospital the Queen paid tribute to the hospital workers, some of whom had been bombed out of their homes and yet continued to work long shifts on the wards.

Buckingham Palace Bombed

Above: Buckingham Palace was bombed on the night of September 13, 1940 and the chapel building was destroyed.

Opposite above: The King and Queen toured the devastation at the Palace. As a gesture of solidarity with the people of London, the King and Queen continued to reside at Buckingham Palace during the War.

Opposite below left: Accompanied by her husband and Prime Minister Winston Churchill, the Queen spoke to workers who were helping to clear up after the bombing.

Opposite below right: The bombing of Buckingham Palace was part of the wider London Blitz that caused severe damage and loss of life across the city. The Queen visited the East End of London and chatted with those who had been affected.

Princesses at War

Opposite above: Suggestions had been made that the Princesses be sent abroad to Canada where it was safer, but the King and Queen did not want to split the family and believed the Princesses should share in the wartime experience of the nation. They were evacuated to their wartime home, where they were pictured taking the dog for an outing in July 1940.

Opposite below: In 1940, at just fourteen years of age, Elizabeth made her first radio broadcast. Her address was aimed at the children of Britain and the Commonwealth, especially those who had been evacuated.

Below: The Princesses helped the war effort by collecting the harvest at Sandringham. Here they are pictured talking to one of the young farmworkers.

Right: The Queen addressed the nation in November 1939 to reassure the mothers of evacuated children.

Queen Mary's War

Opposite below: George V's widow Queen Mary joined in with the war effort. Here she is pictured inspecting the Ship's Company in the West Country in 1941.

Above left: On a visit to Calne in Wiltshire, she met with a group of workers from the Y.M.C.A.

Opposite above: Queen Mary also visited the Y.M.C.A. in Cheltenham where she paused for a cup of tea and shared a joke.

Opposite center: The Queen asked the instructor, who was teaching a class of soldiers, how to cook runner beans.

Left: The Queen posed for a photograph during her tour of the West Country.

Above right: The Queen met a group of children at Queen Mary's Home for Children in Aldershot.

Inspecting the Troops

Opposite below: Princess Elizabeth accompanied her parents on an inspection of the Household Cavalry at barracks in southern England during December 1940.

Opposite above: The following year the King inspected the First County of London Battalion of the Home Guard who were charged with guarding Buckingham Palace.

Left: On a visit to Scotland at the end of January 1941, the Duke of Kent paid a visit of inspection to the Queen's Own Royal West Kent Regiment, of which he was Colonel-in-Chief. Dressed in Air Force uniform, he is pictured inspecting a batallion Guard of Honor.

Above left: The King spent a day in March 1941 with Canadian troops, here traveling on a Bren gun carrier bearing the name "Hell's Angels."

Above right: In September 1941, after conducting a number of inspections, the King and Queen took a break at Balmoral. While there, they attended a service at Crathie Church in honor of National Prayer Day.

Death of the Duke of Kent

Opposite above: The Duke of Kent examined the devastation caused by fire resulting from heavy bombing in January 1941.

Opposite below left: On the same tour of the devastation in London, the Duke talked with a sergeant who was helping with the clear-up.

Opposite below right: In August the Duke was in Canada to inspect the Canadian Air Force at the Jackson Building in Ottawa. After the inspection he was photographed with his uncle, the Governor-General, on the garden lawn at Rideau Hall.

Above: On August 25, 1942 the Duke was killed in a plane crash. Here his body is carried by Royal Air Force service men to an ambulance, which transported the coffin to the Albert Memorial Chapel at Windsor Castle, where the body lay until the funeral.

Left: The Duke's funeral was held on August 30, 1942. Here the Chief Constable of Buckinghamshire offered his sympathies to the Duchess of Kent after leaving the memorial ceremony.

Visiting Dignitaries

Opposite above: During the War, a number of dignitaries from allied and friendly governments visited the King and Queen. Here Eleanor Roosevelt, the First Lady of the United States, is pictured during her stay with the Royal Family.

Above: Here the King and Queen are pictured at a reception celebrating the centenary of New Zealand as a British Colony at Mansion House in February 1940 attended by dignitaries from that country.

Right: The King and the Prime Minister met representatives from across the world at the Dominion, Colonial and Allied Conference at St. James's Palace in June 1941.

Opposite below: On United Nations Day in 1942, the Kings of Norway and Yugoslavia took the salute with the British Royal Family.

The Princesses Pitch In

Opposite below: In April 1942 Elizabeth celebrated her sixteenth birthday by making her first appearance in public at an official ceremony. As Colonel-in-Chief, she reviewed the Grenadier Guards at a special birthday parade of her regiment at Winsdor Castle.

Opposite above: Elizabeth (left) and Margaret purchased the first two Savings Certificates of the new £1 issue at the Post Office in January 1943.

Below right: Elizabeth (left), as the patrol leader of the Buckingham Palace Girl Guides writes a message for Lady Baden-Powell at Guide Headquarters on the occasion of "Thinking Day" in 1943.

Left: The message was sent to Lady Baden-Powell by Pigeon Post. Here Elizabeth carefully attaches the letter to the pigeon.

Below left: Elizabeth (right) and Margaret follow the bird as it flies off into the distance toward Guide Headquarters.

Meeting the Forces

Left: In April 1942 the King spent time watching planes take off and listening to Air Force operations. Here he meets an airman who has just landed and is still wearing his "Mae West."

Opposite below: The King was introduced to some airmen in June 1942.

Opposite above: In a sign of international solidarity, the King inspected a detachment of the Greek Navy at Chatham in Kent.

Below: Dressed in naval uniform, the King listened to the matron of Norwich Hospital give her account of the bombing of the hospital in October 1942.

Giving Thanks

Right: In May 1943 the Royal Family attended a service of thanksgiving at St. Paul's Cathedral in honor of Allies' successes in North Africa.

Below: When leaving the service at St. Paul's the Royal Family were preceded by the Sword of State.

Opposite: Earlier in the year the King had watched England and Wales play a friendly soccer match at Wembley Stadium. Here he is pictured meeting Brian Jones of Wales.

Elizabeth Turns 18

Opposite below: Princess Elizabeth with her parents on her 18th birthday in April 1944.

Opposite above: The Royal Family gathered to celebrate her birthday with a family luncheon hosted by the King and Queen.

Left: After turning 18, Elizabeth began to take on even more Royal duties. Here she makes a speech in June 1944.

Below: A picture of Elizabeth inspecting her former Auxiliary Territorial Service companions when she returned to the Motor Transport Training Center in Camberley, Surrey. She wore the rank of Junior Commander for the first time.

The King Prepares for D-Day

Above: In May 1944, the King, Queen, and Princess Elizabeth spent a day with Airborne troops, expected to be amongst Britain's invasion forces. The King is pictured meeting a parachutist who had been caught-up under a plane and had hung there for twenty minutes before being pulled back inside and jumping again.

Right: The King is kept informed of the latest progress of the invasion force at a naval base in southern England in November 1944.

Opposite above: The Chief of Staff, Commodore G. Bellars, points out the latest naval movements.

Opposite below: With so many troops fighting abroad and with so many having lost their lives, the King's Christmas Day broadcast to the nation in 1944 was especially poignant.

Wartime Family Life

Right: Despite the war, family life continued for the Royals. Here the Princesses arrive at Westminster Abbey for the marriage of Lady Anne Spencer in February 1944.

Opposite above left and right: Sea Ranger Princess Elizabeth shared the chores before setting off in a rowing boat in July 1944.

Opposite below: Prince Richard, the second son of the Duke and Duchess of Gloucester, was born in August 1944. The Queen, Queen Mary, and the Duchess are pictured after the christening.

Below: The King and Queen went to Euston Station to see the Duke and Duchess of Gloucester off on their voyage to Australia, where he was to become Governor General.

Anglo-American Relations

Below: In October 1944 the King paid a visit to France to inspect troops and honor the liberation by Allied forces.

Right: On the trip the King was introduced to the Allies supreme commander, the American General Dwight Eisenhower.

Opposite left: After the war was over, the King met with President Truman aboard H.M.S. *Renown* in Plymouth Sound. The meeting took place very close to the Mayflower Steps, from where the Pilgrim Fathers set sail for New England in 1620.

Opposite right: Highlighting close Anglo-American relations the King was welcomed aboard the U.S.S. *Augusta*, where he inspected the ship's company with its Captain, J. H. Foskett.

War is Over

Right: A famous image of the Royal Family and the Prime Minister acknowledging the crowds from the balcony at Buckingham Palace on Victory in Europe Day.

Honoring the War Effort

Opposite above: In May 1945, soon after the end of the war, the King and Queen made another visit to the East End of London. Here they are pictured on Vallance Road in Stepney.

Opposite below: The King and Queen met wounded soldiers across the country after the war, here they talk to a group of men in Preston.

Below: The King visited Indian soldiers who had recently been released from German prison camps and were resting in Norfolk, awaiting transport back to India.

Left: George VI presented soldiers with the King's Medal at Mansion House in October 1945. Here the King awards a medal to Kenneth Wood.

Victory in Japan

Opposite above: The King celebrated victory over Japan in the grounds of Buckingham Palace after the State Opening of Parliament. He met politicians and generals, including the new Prime Minister, Clement Attlee (third from left).

Left: Just before the Japanese surrender, the Queen paid a visit to St. Mary's Hospital in Paddington, where she toured the innoculation department and was treated to a look at fully grown mold through a microscope.

Opposite below: The Duchess of Kent inspected the Alexandra Day proceedings in 1945. The day commemorates the arrival of Queen Alexandra in Britain in 1863 and roses are sold for charity to mark the anniversary. Here the Duchess is pictured at a rose stall at Holborn Town Hall.

Below: The King and Queen toured Swansea in November 1945 and are welcomed by the Mayor at the Civic Center, after a visit to an oil refinery at Llandarcy.

A Silver Cup for the Princesses

Below left: In May 1945 the Princesses won the silver cup for the best single turn out at the Royal Windsor Horse Show.

Left: Elizabeth continued her inspections of the troops. Here she makes an address after inspecting the Grenadier Guards at the Wellington Barracks.

Below right: Elizabeth leaves the clubhouse of the Association of Girls Clubs and Mixed Clubs in Devonshire Street, London.

Opposite: Elizabeth planted a red oak in Windsor Great Park to commemorate the work done for the Red Cross by the British Agriculture and Allied interests.

Getting Back to Normal

Opposite below: After the war had ended the King and Queen returned to their regular duties. The King was introduced to the soccer players of Charlton Athletic ahead of the Cup Final game at Wembley in April 1946. This fixture was particularly important because it was the first time the tournament had been held since the outbreak of the war.

Right: The Queen and Queen Mary admire an exhibit at the Regency Exhibition at the Brighton Pavilion in July 1946.

Opposite above left: The King and Queen gave their support to the rejuvenation of British industry by visiting the "Britain Can Make it" Exhibition in September 1946. They are pictured with a leather traveling case, one of many consumer goods that the exhibition sought to showcase.

Below: The King and the Queen took particular interest in a young woodworker on a tour of Slough Social Center in December 1947.

Opposite above right: On the same tour of Slough Social Center, the King and Queen have a game of darts. The Queen beat the King by two points after three throws.

South Africa

Above left: The Royal Family headed for South Africa in January 1947. Here they are pictured arriving at Waterloo Station before departure.

Left: They had a busy schedule, but managed to get away for a short break in the Natal National Park.

Above right: Princess Elizabeth turned 21 while the Royal Family was in South Africa. She broadcasts a speech from Cape Town to mark the occasion.

Opposite: The Royal Family were away for several months and did not return until May 1947. A large crowd gathered at Buckingham Palace to welcome them home. The Royals can be seen on the Palace balcony.

Elizabeth Weds

Opposite: In November 1947, at the age of 21, Princess Elizabeth (pictured here arriving for the ceremony) was married to Philip, who became Duke of Edinburgh after the wedding.

Above: The wedding party was photographed at Buckingham Palace after the ceremony at Westminster Abbey.

Left: The newly-weds greeted the crowds of well-wishers from the balcony at Buckingham Palace.

Overleaf: The crowned heads of Europe joined members of the Royal Family to celebrate the wedding.

Silver Wedding Anniversary

Above: April 1948 marked the 25th wedding anniversary of the King and Queen. The family celebrated with a visit to St. Paul's Cathedral (pictured overleaf). After the service they appeared on the balcony at Buckingham Palace to wave to the large crowd that had amassed outside.

Opposite below: The following month, the King and Queen visited the British Industries Fair at Earls Court with Harold Wilson, the President of the Board of Trade. They attended the heavy industries section of the fair in Birmingham a few days later.

Right: The King and Queen attended the wedding of Elizabeth's lady-in-waiting, Lady Margaret Egerton, in October 1948. She married the Princess's private secretary, John Colville. Princess Margaret was a bridesmaid.

Scotland

Opposite above: The Royal Family were in Scotland in July 1948, where they visited the Northern Infirmary in Inverness.

Left: They also visited the Lord Roberts' Memorial Center in Inverness where they spoke with a furniture maker.

Below right: Lord Lovat guided the King and Queen around a highland show.

Below left: At the show, the King and Queen inspected a prize-winning bull.

Opposite below: On the same tour, the Royal party continued with the animal theme and watched a parade of ponies with the Minister of Agriculture, Tom Williams.

Golf and the Olympics

Above: During his trip to Scotland the King drove from Edinburgh to attend the Open Golf Championship at Muirfield.

Right: Here the King pauses for a cigarette during play at Muirfield.

Opposite below: In August 1948, London hosted the first post-war Olympics. The King and Queen watched athletics at Wembley on the Queen's 48th birthday.

Opposite above: The King, Queen, and other spectators stand for the anthem at the London Olympics.

Birth of Prince Charles

Above: On November 14, 1948, Princess Elizabeth gave birth to her first son, Charles Philip Arthur George. Before the announcement was made, excited crowds gathered outside Buckingham Palace.

Right: The news the crowd had been waiting for was delivered in the form of this bulletin, written by the Princess's doctors and posted on the gates of Buckingham Palace.

Opposite above left: The *Daily Mail's* front page on the day of Prince Charles's christening.

Opposite above right: The Edinburgh sky was aglow with good wishes for the baby Prince.

Opposite below: The young prince out for a stroll with his nanny in October 1949.

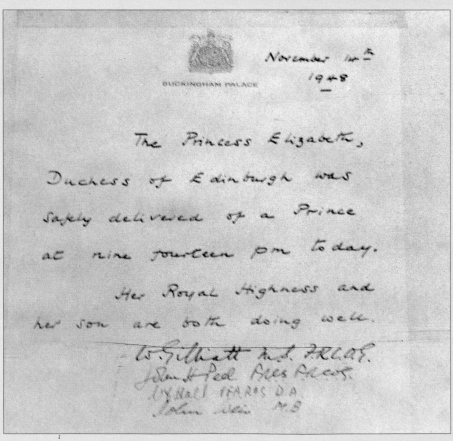

The Braemar Games

Opposite: The King and Queen, dressed in tartan, visited Scotland in September 1948 and opened the Braemar Highland Gathering. It was an important occasion because it marked the centenary of the Royal Family's patronage of the games.

Above: The Braemer Gathering was always popular with the King and Queen and they opened the Games again the following year. Here they are pictured with the Marquess of Aberdeen.

Left: While attending the Games in 1949, the Royal Family, including a young Prince Charles, stayed at Balmoral. They are pictured at Ballater Station on their way to Balmoral.

Watching Soccer

Opposite above left: The King and Queen arriving at the Army Cup Final held at Aldershot in March 1950.

Opposite below: The following month, the King was back in the stands to watch the Football Association Cup final at Wembley. The King is being introduced to Denis Compton of Arsenal.

Opposite above right: The Queen and Princess Margaret during an inspection of an Australian ship.

Right: In May 1950 the King and Queen toured the Chelsea Flower Show at the Royal Hospital in Chelsea.

Below: They visited the Master Mariners Company Ship on the Thames Embankment at Temple Steps in October 1950.

Festival of Britain

Opposite below: The Royal Family visited the South Bank site of the Festival of Britain in May 1951. The South Bank of the River Thames had been completely regenerated as part of the Festival.

Opposite above: The King is pictured signing the visitors' book at the Festival of Britain site.

Below right: Even the 84 year-old Queen Mary visited the exhibition with her two grandsons, Prince William of Gloucester and Prince Michael of Kent.

Below left: The following week the King and Queen were invited to dinner at the Danish Embassy by the Danish monarchs.

Right: The Royal Family at Ascot races in 1951.

The Young Princes

Right: Prince Charles enjoyed his first visit to an airport at two-and-a-half years old, when he went to greet his mother on her return from Malta. He is seen holding the Princess's hand after she had disembarked from the airplane.

Opposite: While being taken for a walk, Prince Charles shows an interest in one of the Coldstream Guards on duty at Clarence House in August 1951.

Above: Prince Charles and Prince Richard were taken for a stroll through Green Park in November 1951.

The King's Last Trip to Balmoral

Opposite below: In August 1951 the Royal Family arrived at Ballater Station to start their summer holiday at Balmoral.

Opposite above left: Ballater Station: The Queen with Prince Charles and Princess Anne, who was born the year before on August 15, 1950.

Above: The King and Queen returned to the Braemar Gathering in September 1951 with Princess Margaret and the Duke of Edinburgh.

Left: George Clark was presented to the King and Queen after "Tossing the Caber" at the Braemer Games.

Opposite above right: The King returned from Scotland ahead of the rest of the Royal Family after his medical advisers suggested he have a thorough medical check-up. He is pictured here in the car traveling between Euston Station and Buckingham Palace.

The Death of King George VI

Below: The *Daily Mail*'s last photograph of the King was taken at London Airport where he had been saying goodbye to Princess Elizabeth as she departed on an Australian tour.

Right: The King died on February 6, 1952. This is how the event was covered by the *Evening Standard*.

Opposite above: On the day of his death, the Honourable Artillery Company fired one shot per minute for each of the 56 years of the King's life. A similar salute was given in Hyde Park.

Opposite below: Crowds gathered at Buckingham Palace gates to pay their respects.

Below right: The lights at the normally vibrant Piccadilly Circus were turned off as a mark of respect.

Evening Standard — Wednesday, February 6, 1952

THE KING DIES IN HIS SLEEP

A peaceful end this morning

The Evening Standard announces with deep regret that the King died early this morning.

The announcement came from Sandringham at 10.45 a.m. It said: "The King, who retired to rest last night in his usual health, passed peacefully away in his sleep early this morning."

With him at Sandringham were the Queen, Princess Margaret and the King's grandchildren, Prince Charles and Princess Anne.

The King was 56. It is 136 days since the operation on his lung. Yesterday he was out rabbit shooting for several hours. To everybody he appeared to be in the very best of health.

To-day he had planned to go out shooting hares. But when gamekeepers went to Sandringham House for instructions they were told: "The shoot is cancelled."

One doctor was called to Sandringham before the announcement of the King's death was made. He was 37-year-old Dr. James Ansell, local man who held the title of Surgeon Apothecary to the Sandringham Household.

News of her father's death was telephoned to Princess Elizabeth, the new Sovereign, in Africa. She decided to fly home immediately.

She is due to arrive at 4.30 p.m. to-morrow and will meet the Privy Council to give orders for Court mourning and the funeral.

By then she will have been proclaimed Queen—at an Accession Council at St. James's Palace at five o'clock this evening.

The story of the King's last shoot was told this afternoon by one of his party, Lord Fermoy.

He said: "Yesterday was one of the loveliest winter days I have ever known in Norfolk.

"It was perfect for shooting and the King was ready to move off soon after 9.30.

This is the picture that first told the people of Britain that all was not well with the King. It was taken on May 2 last year, when the King was driving back to Buckingham.

The new Queen flies home to-night

From EVELYN IRONS: Nyeri, Wednesday

Princess Elizabeth heard the news of her father's death 45 minutes after the announcement from Sandringham.

She was told by Prince Philip. A member of her household said: "She stood it very bravely, like a Queen."

Arrangements were made immediately for the Princess and the Prince to fly home to-night.

The news was telephoned to the Royal Lodge by a Nairobi newspaper.

It was decided to withhold it until direct confirmation was obtained from Buckingham Palace.

Palace call

Soon afterwards a direct radio-telephone call came through from the Royal Family.

The call was routed to the Princess through a little country post office in the Kenya countryside.

It took nearly 30 minutes for the call to be properly connected and established from London.

Then the Princess and the Prince left the Royal Lodge here by car and drove to the airfield at Nanyuki where a Dakota of East African Airways waited to fly them to Entebbe, Uganda.

6.30 p.m. take-off

They were taking off at 6.30 p.m. from Entebbe, Uganda, for home in the
● Page Two, Col. Four

LYING IN STATE NEXT WEEK

At Westminster Hall

The body of the King will be taken to Westminster Hall, probably this week-end. It will lie in state on a catafalque in the centre of the hall throughout next week, beginning on Monday. A guard will be maintained night and day.

The funeral is expected to take place early in the following week.

Parliament will be adjourned until after the funeral, probably for ten days or a fortnight.

ONE PROGRAMME ON BBC AND ALL SHOWS CLOSE

Shops clear gay windows

The announcement of the King's death was made on the BBC at 11.15 a.m. Announcer John Snagge added: "The BBC offers profound sympathy to Her Majesty the Queen and the Royal Family."

Then the BBC closed down for the rest of the day except for news, special bulletins, shipping forecasts and gale warnings.

A short sombre air was broadcast at 6 to-night.

The Home and Light programmes are to merge until after the funeral. To-morrow serious music will be broadcast on all stations.

On Friday some other sustaining programmes will be resumed, but a single programme will be sent out for the next two days.

The overseas broadcasts will give serious music for the next 24 hours with news and special bulletins. Programmes go back to normal after the funeral.

The television service announced the news then closed on the demonstration film at 11.30 a.m.

At 11.45 screens showed the BBC coat of arms with the
▲ Page Two, Col. Five

WEATHER—Cloudy

The Funeral of King George VI

Opposite below left: Floral tributes amassed in the grounds of Windsor Castle.

Opposite below right: A close-up of the cortège with the coffin as it passed down Horse Guards Parade.

Opposite above: The King's body lying-in-state in Westminster Hall. Four gold candelabra from Westminster Abbey stand at the four corners of the coffin, which was guarded continuously by officers of the Household Troops; Members of the King's Bodyguard and the King's Gentlemen at Arms. The body remained in the Hall for three days, allowing members of the public to file past the coffin.

Above: People paid their final respects to the King as his coffin proceeded toward his final resting place in St. George's Chapel, Windsor.

Left: Preceded by the sound of the Trumpeters of the State Heralds, the Garter King at Arms read the first public proclamation of the accession of Queen Elizabeth II from the balcony at Friary Court, St. James's Palace on February 8, 1952.

The Coronation of Queen Elizabeth II

Above left: Elizabeth was officially crowned Queen on June 2, 1953 at Westminster Abbey, with some 8000 people in attendance, whilst millions more were able to watch the ceremony on television for the first time. She begins her journey to the Abbey in the Gold State Coach.

Above right: Wearing a simple white dress, the Queen is seated in St. Edward's Chair, surrounded by Knights of the Garter as she prepares for the Ceremony of the Anointing.

Right: She bears the Rod with Dove, symbol of equity and mercy in her left hand, and the Scepter with Cross, the symbol of power and justice, in her right, whilst the Archbishop of Canterbury prepares to place St. Edward's Crown on her head.

Opposite: Having spoken private prayers, the Queen takes the Chair of Estate.

Following pages: After the formal proceedings the Queen and her attendants leave Westminster Abbey.

That evening, the Queen appeared on the balcony of Buckingham Palace to greet the cheering crowds that thronged below and to watch the flypast salute by the Royal Air Force.

Family Time

Opposite above: A year after the Coronation the Queen's official birthday was marked by the Royal Air Force with an official flypast. Princess Anne and Prince Charles joined Princess Margaret and the Queen Mother.

Opposite below: The family again gathered on the balcony that year as crowds gathered to chant birthday wishes to the Duke of Edinburgh during the Trooping the Color ceremony.

Left: A chance for the Queen to spend time playing with Princess Anne and her pony Greensleeves during the family summer holiday in Balmoral.

Formal Occasions

Opposite: Elizabeth arrived at Victoria Palace for the annual Royal Variety Show in November 1955.

Left: Swathed in white fur, the Queen attended the Order of the Bath Ceremony in Westminster Abbey the following year.

Below: Guests milled across the lawn during the Royal Garden Party at Buckingham Palace.

Bottom: During a Royal visit to Nigeria in 1956, she greeted guests at another garden party, this time in the grounds of Government House, Enugu.

Passion for Horses

Above and center: A chance for the Queen and Duke of Edinburgh to spend a family day together with Prince Charles and Princess Anne at a polo match in 1956.

Below: In the same year the Queen and Duke made a Royal visit to South Uist and Benbecula in Scotland. The Duke drove to the proposed site of the North Ford bridge.

Opposite above: At Epsom races the Queen Mother took the opportunity to walk to the paddock before the start of the Derby. She was accompanied by the Earl of Rosebery.

Opposite below left: The Queen and Duke of Edinburgh walked in procession to Windsor Castle for the service of the Order of the Garter in St. George's Chapel.

Opposite below right: The Queen and Princess Margaret spoke to jockey Dick Francis at Aintree. He was about to ride the Queen Mother's horse, Devon Loch.

Royal Visit to Guernsey

Opposite above left: During a visit to St. Peter's Port in Guernsey, Elizabeth was presented with a bouquet by Hilary Beacher, aged 13.

Opposite above right: She also visited Elizabeth College on the island where six thousand children sang her a "song of welcome" much to her obvious delight.

Opposite below left: In 1957 the World Scouts Jamboree took place in Sutton Park in Warwickshire. The Queen visited the site and is pictured as she passes the arch of the Iranian scouts, one of the features of the camp.

Opposite below right: The Queen just after she had broadcast her Christmas Day message to the nation in 1957.

Left: Children climbed onto the St. Albans Abbey window sills to watch the Queen and Prince Philip leave after a church service.

Below left: Proud parents, accompanied by his sister Princess Anne, watched as Prince Charles (fourth from left of the competitors) took part in a race at his school sports day in Chelsea, London.

Below right: Prince Charles and Princess Anne in December 1957.

Supporting the Arts

Above: In November 1958, the Queen attended a dinner held at the American Embassy in London, hosted by the American Vice-President, Richard Nixon.

Right: Later in the year, she was present at the Odeon, Leicester Square for the premiere of Danny Kaye's movie *Me and the Colonel*, where guests included Nicole Maurey and Mr and Mrs Kurt Jurgens.

Opposite above left: Prince Charles on his way to see a gala performance of *The Nutcracker* given in aid of the Royal Ballet Benevolent Fund at the Royal Opera House, Covent Garden, London.

Opposite above right: The Queen with Lord Mountbatten at the premiere of *Dunkirk* in 1958. This was the same month in which the last debutantes would be presented before her at the Royal Court.

Opposite below: During the summer of 1959 the Queen visited the Royal Botanical Gardens at Kew, which celebrated its bicentenary. She visited the refurbished Palm House and took tea in the Orangery.

At Windsor Castle

Opposite and left: The Queen and Duke of Edinburgh enjoy the chance to relax in the grounds of Windsor Castle, just prior to setting off for a tour of North America.

Below left: Ten-year-old Princess Anne was clutching a two-feet long doll dressed in Welsh costume when she arrived at Cardiff Docks to board the royal yacht *Britannia*. The Royal Family was due to set off for a cruise around the Orkney and Shetland islands. She had been presented with the doll by the Arts and Crafts section on a visit to the Eisteddford.

Below right: Despite the rain, the Queen and Duke cheerfully greeted the crowds at Royal Ascot in 1960.

Princess Margaret Marries

Right: Two days before their marriage, the radiant bride-to-be left Clarence House with her fiancé to attend a reception ball at Buckingham Palace. Two thousand well-wishers greeted them in The Mall.

Below left and right: On May 6, 1960 Princess Margaret left Clarence House with the Duke of Edinburgh who was to give her away. They made the journey to Westminster Abbey, where she was to marry Antony Armstrong-Jones.

Opposite: The magnificent wedding ceremony at Westminster Abbey was conducted by the Archbishop of Canterbury, Dr. Geoffrey Fisher. The bride was accompanied by her eight bridesmaids and Dr. Roger Gilliat was best man.

The Newlyweds

Above left: The wedding ceremony was the first Royal wedding to be televised and was broadcast to over twenty million people.

Above right: Princess Margaret and Antony Armstrong-Jones enter their coach after the ceremony.

Right: They traveled in the Queen's coach which was cheered by the crowds as it passed down The Mall.

Opposite above and below: The newlyweds went out onto the balcony at Buckingham Palace to greet the cheering well-wishers that thronged into The Mall. They were joined by other members of the Royal Family.

Honeymooners

Opposite above: Princess Margaret and Antony Armstrong-Jones acknowledge the delighted crowds below.

Opposite below: The thousands lining The Mall surged forward in their enthusiasm to greet the newly-married couple.

Left: After the celebrations the Royal Family rushed forward to give the happy couple a rose petal send-off before they embarked on their honeymoon on the Royal Yacht *Britannia* to cruise around the Caribbean.

Below: The young Princess Anne was amongst the eight bridesmaids and can be seen to the left of the Queen and Queen Mother. Guests waved goodbye from the Palace forecourt as the newlyweds departed for their honeymoon.

Baby Prince Andrew

Above: The Queen Mother holds the infant Prince Andrew on her 60th birthday at Clarence House. Prince Charles and Princess Anne were also there to enjoy the celebrations. He was born on February 19, 1960.

Right: The Queen Mother, accompanied by Prince Charles and Princess Anne watched the veterinary inspection at the stables of Badminton House on the final day of the Badminton Horse Trials.

Opposite above left: Princess Margaret was one of the members of the Royal Family invited to dine with the King and Queen of Siam at the Thai Embassy in London.

Opposite above right: Princess Margaret and Antony Armstrong-Jones left King's Cross Station to take a train to Balmoral in August 1960 amid speculation that she was expecting a baby, which proved to be unfounded.

Opposite below left: Prince Charles at the the three-day Badminton Horse Trials.

Opposite below right: The Queen spends time with her eldest son at the trials.

Overleaf: Precious family time at Balmoral as they all enjoy playing with baby Prince Andrew.

Duke of Kent Marries

Right: In June 1961 the Queen met the new President of the United States of America, John F. Kennedy and his wife, Jackie, at a reception held at Buckingham Palace.

Opposite above left: In the same month, the Duke of Kent was married to Miss Katharine Worsley. He wore the uniform of his regiment, the Royal Scots Guards.

Opposite above right: Princess Margaret and her husband, Antony Armstrong-Jones, attended the Duke of Kent's wedding. In October Armstrong-Jones was to accept the title Earl of Snowdon.

Opposite below left: The Queen attended the three-day horse trials at Badminton.

Opposite below right: In July, the Queen presented the John Player trophy to Pat Smythe, the winner of the International Horse Show-jumping Competition.

Royal Duties

Above left: The family gather for the Trooping the Color ceremony in 1962. A young Prince Andrew waves to the crowds.

Above right: The Queen leaves the London Palladium after watching the *Royal Variety Show*.

Right: Later in the year she was present for the premiere of *Lawrence of Arabia* at the Leicester Square Odeon.

Opposite above left: The Queen at London Airport just before flying to Holland.

Opposite above right: A chance for mother and daughter to look round at Badminton.

Opposite below left: In October 1962 the Queen greeted the stars at the Royal Command Performance held at the London Palladium. She can be seen shaking hands with Cliff Richard, who stands alongside Harry Secombe and Eartha Kitt.

Opposite below right: The following year she presented the Championship Trophy to Rod Laver, winner of the Men's Singles Competition at Wimbledon.

Royal Tour

Above: At the beginning of 1963 the Queen and Prince Philip left London Airport to take part in a Royal tour of Fiji, Australia, and New Zealand.

Opposite above left: While in Melbourne, Australia, the Queen visited the Royal Children's Hospital.

Opposite above right: The Queen photographed in New Zealand during the tour.

Opposite below: At the end of the eight-week tour the Queen Mother and Princess Anne were at London Airport to welcome them home. They drove to Windsor where Prince Charles joined them later that day having just begun his Easter vacation from Gordonstoun School.

Right: The Queen and Duke at the Order of the Garter ceremony at Windsor in June 1963.

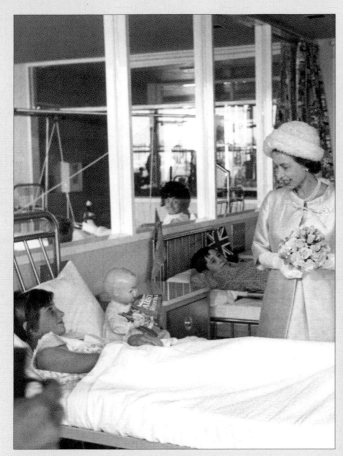

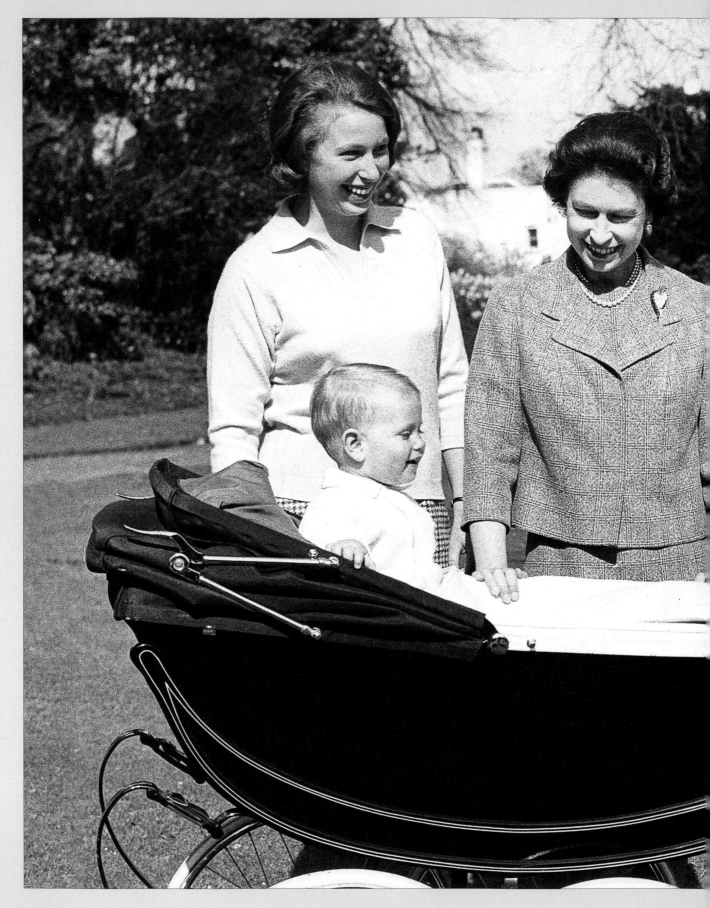

Welcome Prince Edward

Previous page and above: Prince Edward was born on March 10, 1964. On the Queen's 39th birthday she spent time with her family at Frogmore House which is situated in Home Park, below Windsor Castle.

Right: The Queen was introduced to the comedian Ken Dodd at the *Royal Variety Performance* held at the London Palladium. Dudley Moore, Spike Milligan, and Max Bygraves are also pictured.

A Visit to the Isle of Wight

Left: In July 1965 Elizabeth II became the first reigning monarch since 1671 to make an official visit to the Isle of Wight. At Carisbrooke Castle she installed Earl Mountbatten as "Governor and Captain of All Our Isle of Wight."

Below left: Later that month the Queen attended the Gala performance of *Tosca* at Covent Garden.

Below right: In November 1966 the Queen visited the Royal Albert Hall for the St. Celia Festival Royal Charity Concert.

Trains and Planes

Opposite above left: Queen Elizabeth arrives at Buckingham station for a tour of Buckinghamshire.

Opposite above right: Prince Edward is anxious to board the Royal train as he tugs at the Queen's hand before they head from London to Balmoral.

Opposite below left: The Queen in Belfast, Northern Ireland in July 1966.

Opposite below right: The Queen accompanies the Marquess of Exeter in the front seat of a Land Rover at the Burghley Horse Trials World Championships.

Left: In September 1966 she visited the British Aircraft Corporation Works in Filton, Bristol but was late leaving due to her interest in the progress of the Anglo-French Concorde project.

Below left: The Queen Mother and Viscount Linley, Princess Margaret's son, on their way to a church service at Crathie Church near Balmoral.

Below right: Prince Philip, Princess Anne, and Prince Charles on their return from Jamaica.

A Family Reunion

Above: A momentous occasion in the family's history when the Queen met the Duke of Windsor for the first time since his abdication thirty years previously. They had joined together to unveil a plaque in memory of Queen Mary, the Duke's mother and the Queen's grandmother. (Left to right: The Queen Mother, the Duke and Duchess of Gloucester, the Duke and Duchess of Windsor, The Queen).

Opposite above left: An elementary school in Hungerford Road, Islington received a visit from the Queen in February 1967.

Opposite above right: Princess Anne congratulated Betty Janaway and attached a rosette to her horse Grey Leg. They had just won the Queen Elizabeth II Cup at the Royal International Horse Show at White City.

Opposite below left: The annual Order of the Garter ceremony at Windsor.

Opposite below right: With an amused expression, the Queen watches the parade at Epsom races just before the start of the Derby. She is accompanied by the Duchess of Gloucester (center) and the Queen Mother.

Left: The Queen signs the visitors' book after a visit to the Naval and Military Club.

Happy Birthday

Opposite: The Royal Family pictured at Windsor on the Queen's 42nd birthday in 1968.

Above left: The Queen met Joan Collins and William Dix at the premiere of *Doctor Doolittle* at the Odeon, Leicester Square.

Left: At the end of 1968, the Queen, who had recently returned from a visit to South America, attended a service at St. George's Chapel, Windsor, with Princess Anne. They were met by the Dean of Windsor, the Very Reverend John Woods. Later, to mark the 50th anniversary of the Royal Air Force, the Queen was presented with a pair of large silver candlesticks.

Above right: Prince Charles deep in conversation with government minister, Barbara Castle, during a visit to her department. He was on vacation from Cambridge University at the time.

Above: Both Prince Charles and Princess Anne attended the gala performance of *The Nutcracker* given in aid of the Royal Ballet Benevolent Fund at the Royal Opera House, Covent Garden.

Prince of Wales

Opposite: 1969 was perhaps more significant and daunting for Prince Charles than for any other member of the Royal Family, as it was to be the year of his investiture as the Prince of Wales, a fact that was met with considerable resistance by Welsh Nationalists, who saw the ceremony as an act of English oppression. In an attempt to diffuse hostile opinion, the Prince spent a semester at the University of Aberystwyth in Wales and a series of photographs was published to show him in a more informal light. However, on July 1, the morning of the ceremony itself, two men were killed as they attempted to plant a bomb near Caernarvon Castle.

Left: Prince Charles as he travels to Caernarvon Castle for the ceremony.

Below: After the investiture the Queen takes the new Prince of Wales to King's Gate to present him to his people. He was also presented to the people outside Queen Eleanor's Gate and within the Lower Ward of the castle.

Church Service

Above left: The newly-invested Prince of Wales seen here soon after the occasion.

Opposite: Prince Charles leaves a church service with the Queen Mother and other members of the Royal Family.

Left: Then he was busy conversing with guests at the Royal Garden Party at Buckingham Palace.

Royal Grandchildren and Official Engagements

Below: Christmas 1969 and the ten royal grandchildren are photographed together on the East Terrace at Windsor after the morning service in St. George's Chapel. Left to right: Master James Ogilvy; Lady Sarah Armstrong Jones; the Earl of St. Andrews; Lady Helen Windsor; Prince of Wales; Viscount Linley, Prince Andrew; Miss Marina Ogilvy; Princess Anne, and Prince Edward.

Right: In March 1969 the Queen officially opened the new Victoria Line of the London Underground, and became the first reigning monarch to make a journey on the system.

Opposite above: In February 1969 the Queen and Prince Philip were joined for lunch at Buckingham Palace by the President of the United States, Richard Nixon.

Opposite below: Prince Charles, accompanied his parents and sister to the 25th anniversary Variety Performance, held in aid of the Army Benevolent Fund.

A Day At the Races

Left: Princess Anne at Epsom races seen watching events with Princess Alexandra.

Below left: The Queen celebrates after the running of the Epsom Derby.

Below right: A smiling Princess Anne shies away from the cameras at the racecourse.

Opposite above: The Prince was welcomed by an air hostess as he boarded an Air Canada flight destined for Toronto. He was then due to fly on to Ottawa courtesy of the Canadian Air Force to join other members of the family for a ten-day tour of the North-West Territories.

Opposite below: Princess Margaret and Lord Snowdon left London Airport for a week's tour of Yugoslavia. It was the first official visit by a member of the Royal Family to a Communist country.

The Young Edward

Right: The Queen and her six-year-old son Edward arrive at the Royal Windsor Horse Show. During the visit Prince Edward made his first trophy presentation to a 12-year-old girl who had won the children's pony championship.

Above and far right: The Queen and Princess Anne pictured just before they left for Canada for a ten-day tour. Prince Charles had flown out separately.

Opposite above: Princess Anne, Prince Edward, the Queen Mother, the Prince of Wales, and Lady Sarah Armstrong-Jones drive in an open carriage from Buckingham Palace to watch the Trooping the Color ceremony on Horse Guards Parade.

Opposite below left: The Queen and Prince Edward at Badminton in April 1971. The following year, Princess Anne became European Champion at the three-day horse trials held at Burghley in September, despite an operation to remove an ovarian cyst the month before.

Opposite below right: The family plans their forthcoming trip to Australasia.

The Younger Generation

Opposite above left: The Queen Mother celebrated her 70th birthday at Clarence House with Prince Edward and his young cousins, Lady Sarah and Viscount Linley.

Opposite above right: The Queen, Princess Anne, and Prince Charles seen arriving at the *"Talk of the Town"* for a Royal Gala cabaret in aid of the World Wildlife Fund.

Opposite below left and right: The Queen Mother at the Badminton Horse Trials with her grandchildren Prince Andrew, Viscount Linley, the Earl of St Andrew's (left picture only—shown to the right of the Queen Mother) and Lady Sarah Armstrong-Jones (right picture only—shown on the left).

Left: The Queen and Princess Anne seen leaving Heathrow Airport for the state visit to New Zealand and Australia.

Below: The Queen, Prince Philip, and Prince Edward at the Royal Windsor Horse Show. The pair of grays in the foreground were part of the team entered by the Queen for the three-day driving event.

Charles Receives His "Wings"

After graduating, Prince Charles was to join the Royal Navy. Prior to this, he attended Royal Air Force College Cranwell for some advanced flying training.

Above: The Queen, the Queen Mother, Princess Anne, and Prince Andrew coming ashore in Thurso from the Royal Yacht *Britannia* on Anne's 21st birthday, August 15, 1971. Despite her youth, Anne was now President of the Save the Children Fund.

Right: The Prince of Wales and the Duke of Edinburgh at R.A.F. College Cranwell where the Prince received his "wings."

Opposite below: The Prince of Wales at a charity cricket match during his stay at Cranwell.

Opposite above: The Queen and Prince Philip, with Prince Edward between them and the Queen Mother, Prince Charles, and Princess Anne following, leaving St. George's Chapel, Windsor on Christmas Day.

Silver Wedding

The Queen's uncle, the Duke of Windsor, died in May in Paris. More sadness followed when her 30-year-old cousin, Prince William of Gloucester was killed in an air crash. Later in the year, the Queen and Prince Philip were able to enjoy happier times as they celebrated their silver wedding anniversary in November.

Opposite above: The Royal couple at Balmoral.

Opposite below left: The Queen at Balmoral.

Opposite below right: The Queen visited St. Peter's Church of England School in London as part of their centenary celebrations.

Above: The Queen attended the "Treasures of Tutankhamun" exhibition in London.

Far left: The Queen and Prince Philip attended the"Fanfare for Europe" Gala at Covent Garden to celebrate the country's entry into the Common Market.

Left: Princess Anne and Captain Mark Phillips in the grounds of Buckingham Palace following the announcement of their engagement.

Public Engagements

Opposite left top: Princess Anne at Amberley Horse Show with her new pet dog.

Opposite left middle: Princess Anne competing at a one-day event at Amberley Horse Show, Cirencester.

Opposite left bottom: Princess Anne falling from her horse whilst competing at the European Cross Country Championships in Russia.

Opposite right: The Queen visiting The Boys' and Girls' Brigade Headquarters in London.

Above left: Princess Margaret and Princess Anne attending church at Castle Rising, Norfolk.

Above right: The Queen visited Aberfan Cemetery, Wales, to lay a wreath at the slate memorial cross, commemorating the loss of the 116 children and 28 adults who perished in the 1966 Aberfan disaster.

Left: In March, Eric Morecambe and Ernie Wise met the Queen at the Odeon Leicester Square, whilst attending the preview of *Lost Horizon*.

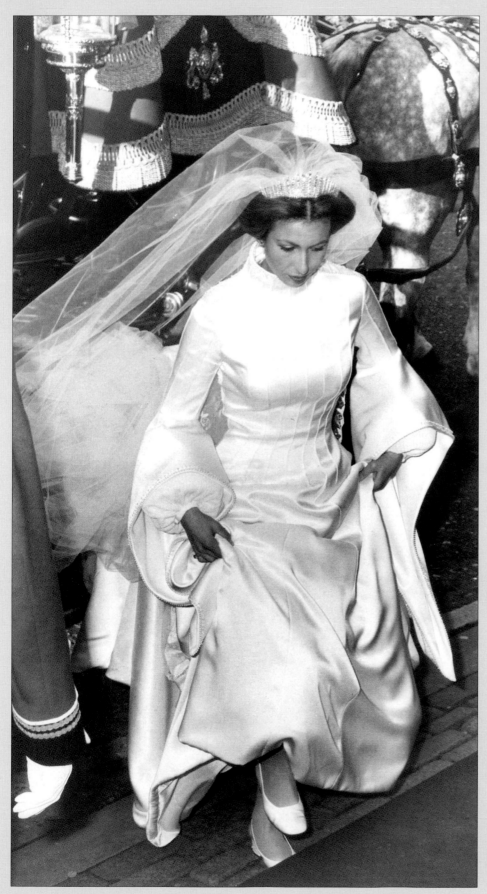

Princess Anne Marries

After an engagement announcement in May, the Queen's only daughter married Captain Mark Phillips on November 14 1973 at Westminster Abbey, watched by over 500 million viewers worldwide.

Left: Princess Anne arriving at Westminster Abbey.

Opposite below left: The Princess and her husband leaving the Abbey after the service.

Opposite above: After the wedding ceremony, the Royal couple greeted well-wishers from the balcony at Buckingham Palace.

Opposite below right: Princess Anne at a show-jumping event.

Royal Duties

Opposite above left: The Queen, Prince Philip, and Princes Andrew and Edward visiting the Duke of Beaufort's hounds.

Opposite above right: The Queen's bodyguard; Her Majesty inspected the bodyguard of the Yeoman of the Guard at Buckingham Palace.

Opposite below left: The Queen attended the Royal Windsor Horse Show with King Constantine of Greece and the husband of Princess Margaretha of Sweden, Mr John Ambler.

Opposite below right and left: The Queen on her 48th birthday at Windsor, where she reviewed the Queen's Scouts.

Above: The Queen visiting the Chelsea Flower Show.

Prince Charles Grows into his Public Role

Both the Prince of Wales and his sister continued to increase their Royal engagements.

Opposite: Prince Charles with the Queen and Princess Alexandra at a production of Alan Ayckbourn's play *Third Person Singular* at the Vaudeville Theatre.

Left: The Queen and the Duke of Edinburgh with Prince Edward at Stratfield Saye House, the home of the Duke of Wellington.

Below left: Princess Anne taking the salute as Chief Commandant of the Women's Royal Naval Service at a passing out parade at H.M.S. *Gauntless* in Burghfield, Berkshire.

Below right: Prince Charles at the British Sub Aqua Club banquet at the Guildhall.

Kidnap Attempt

Whilst on a state visit to Indonesia in March 1974, the Queen received news that Princess Anne and her husband, Mark Phillips, had survived a kidnap attempt whilst being driven down The Mall. Four people received gunshot wounds during the incident, including the Princess's bodyguards and chauffeur.

Opposite above left: Princess Anne and Captain Mark Phillips at the Amberley Horse Trials.

Opposite above right: Princess Anne at the film and TV award celebrations of the Society of Film and Television Arts.

Opposite below: The Queen said "thank-you" to the heroes who helped foil the kidnap attempt by presenting them with gallantry awards.

Above: Policemen combing the sidewalk for a bullet, feet from the spot where Princess Anne's car was forced to stop in the kidnap attempt.

Left: The shattered windshield of a taxi, caught in the incident in The Mall, stands behind a policeman searching for evidence.

A Royal Ride-out

Opposite above left: In the summer, the Queen was introduced to the English cricket team by captain Tony Greig, as they prepared to take on Australia in the Second Test.

Opposite above right: The Queen attended the premiere of *Rooster Cogburn* at the Odeon, Leicester Square. The event was held in aid of the Police Dependents' Trust, and Laura Gisbourne, the daughter of Police Inspector David Gisbourne who had died in the Red Lion riots the previous year, presented the Queen with a bouquet.

Opposite below left: The Queen and Princess Margaret at the Royal Windsor Horse Show.

Opposite below right: The Queen Mother in the grounds of Clarence House on her 75th birthday.

Above: The Queen horse-riding with other members of the Royal Family at Ascot. Captain Mark Phillips and Prince Charles are leading the group, followed by the Queen and Princess Anne.

Left: The Queen with Princess Alexandra and the Duchess of Gloucester at Epsom on Derby Day.

A Royal Separation

The sad news that Princess Margaret and her husband, the Earl of Snowdon, were to separate was made public in March, but this was followed by happier times in April when the Queen celebrated her 50th birthday.

Opposite above left: Crowds greet the Queen at the top of Buster Hill when she officially opened the new Queen Elizabeth Country Park, near Petersfield in August 1976.

Opposite above right: The Queen went with her sons, Prince Charles, Prince Andrew, and Prince Edward at the Montreal Olympic Games to watch her daughter, Princess Anne, compete in the equestrian event.

Opposite below left: The Queen Mother with her grandchildren, (left to right) Viscount Linley, Prince Edward, and Lady Sarah Armstrong-Jones in the grounds of Clarence House on her 76th birthday.

Opposite below right: The Queen at the Badminton Horse Trials with Pipkin the dachshund (who belonged to her sister, Princess Margaret).

Left: Prince Charles at the Powys Game Fair.

The Queen's Silver Jubilee

Opposite: In 1977 the Queen and the country celebrated 25 years of Elizabeth II's reign, and the public demonstrated massive support for the reigning monarch. She undertook an extensive tour of both the United Kingdom and the Commonwealth, during which huge crowds lined the streets and gathered outside Buckingham Palace to show their affection.

Left and below left: The official celebrations began at Windsor in June, with the Queen lighting the first of 100 beacons, and with the Royal Family attending a special service at St. Paul's Cathedral.

Below right: Adoring crowds turned out to see the Queen on her visit to Brighton.

Jubilee Tour

Above: The Queen's Jubilee tour of the country continued in the Channel Islands in 1978. Here the Queen is pictured on walkabout at St. Peter's Port in Guernsey, where huge crowds lined along the narrow streets to see her.

Above right: The Queen pictured at the Badminton Horse Trials in 1978 wearing a raincoat.

Right: The Queen finds great amusement from an incident at the Badminton Horse Trials.

Opposite left: Sitting upon the throne, and wearing her reading glasses, the Queen prepares to deliver her speech at the 1978 State Opening of Parliament. She outlined the plans of the government to try to bring inflation and unemployment under control.

Opposite right above and below: The Queen is pictured clearly enjoying her day out at Epsom races. She was there to see her horse, English Harbour, compete in the Derby.

The Queen in the Middle East

Above left: The Queen arrived in Riyadh, Saudi Arabia at the beginning of 1979 to begin a three-week tour of the Persian Gulf. Upon arriving at the airport she respected the local law and ensured that both her ankles and arms were covered by a long sapphire-blue dress.

Left: While in Bahrain, the Queen attended a racehorse meeing despite the 90 degree heat and the swirling desert winds.

Above right: Back in London, the Queen was in Deptford to celebrate the 250th Anniversary of St Paul's Church.

Opposite above left: (From left to right) Bill Haley, James Galway, and Red Buttons watch as the Queen greets Reginald Bosenquet after the 1979 Royal Variety Performance.

Opposite right: The Queen Mother arriving at the Odeon Leicester Square for a screening of *California Suite*. Princesses Margaret and Anne also joined her for the evening out.

Opposite below left: The Queen gives racing advice to Princess Michael of Kent in the Royal Box at Epsom.

The Death of Lord Mountbatten

Opposite above left: The news of the assassination of Lord Mountbatten (pictured) on August 27, 1979 shook the Royal Family. An IRA bomb, which had been planted on his yacht, killed him and three others, including his 14-year-old grandson.

Right and opposite below left: The funeral of Lord Mountbatten took place at Westminster Abbey with the whole Royal Family in attendance.

Opposite above right: Lord Mountbatten was especially close to Prince Charles as a friend and mentor. This picture indicates some of the emotion the Prince was feeling at the funeral.

Opposite below right: In December, another memorial service was held at St. Paul's Cathedral. Here Princess Margaret and Prince Edward are pictured leaving the service.

Anniversary at Balmoral

Right, below, and opposite: The Queen and the Duke of Edinburgh spent time at Balmoral in November 1979 to celebrate their 32nd wedding anniversary. Their four children accompanied them on the visit as well as their young grandson, Peter Phillips.

The Queen Mother's 80th Birthday

Above right: On August 4, 1980 the Queen Mother turned 80. Here she is pictured on the balcony at Clarence House, where crowds had gathered to sing "Happy Birthday."

Right: Several weeks before the big day, the Queen Mother enjoyed a birthday procession. Members of the Royal Family paraded through the streets in open-top carriages.

Above: Princesses Margaret and Anne were joined in the carriage by Margaret's daughter Sarah Armstrong-Jones.

Opposite above left and right: The Duke and Duchess of Kent (right) and Prince and Princess Michael of Kent (left) in the procession.

Opposite below: The Queen Mother acknowledges the good wishes of the crowds outside Buckingham Palace during her 80th Birthday celebrations.

Lady Diana Spencer

Right: Although they had first met in 1977, it was not until 1980 that a relationship began to blossom between Prince Charles and Lady Diana Spencer, and the media began to take an increasing interest.

Below: When she returned home after a holiday at Balmoral with the Royal Family, she found the press camped outside her London apartment.

Opposite: Diana worked as a kindergarten supervisor, and although not formally trained, demonstrated a natural ability when it came to caring for children.

Charles and Diana

Right: The relationship moved swiftly, and on February 24, 1981, the couple officially announced their engagement.

Opposite above right: Diana's engagement ring consisted of a large sapphire set in white gold, surrounded by 14 diamonds.

Opposite below: Diana soon moved into Buckingham Palace and began to accompany the Prince to official functions and public events. Here she is pictured with Andrew Parker-Bowles at the Horse and Hound Grand Military Gold Cup at Sandown, in which Charles was competing.

Opposite above left: While Charles and Diana prepared for their wedding, Princess Anne gave birth to a baby daughter, Zara Phillips, in May 1981.

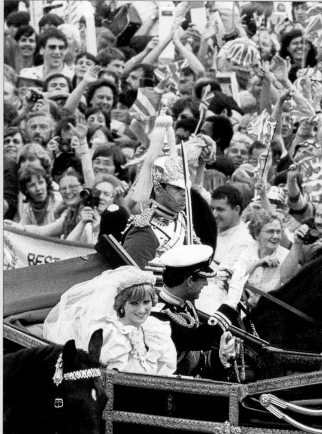

The Royal Wedding

Opposite below: Charles and Diana's wedding was a truly spectacular occasion. The service took place at St. Paul's Cathedral, rather than at Westminster Abbey, as was more traditional, and the day was declared a public holiday. A million people were estimated to have lined the processional route from St. Paul's to Buckingham Palace, whilst some 700 million watched the proceedings on television.

Opposite above left: The newlyweds emerged from the Cathedral to rapturous applause, before proceeding to their waiting coach. Diana's dress had been designed by David and Elizabeth Emanuel and included a 25-foot train.

Opposite above right: Accompanied by a mounted escort, the happy couple were conveyed to Buckingham Palace in their open-topped coach, where a huge crowd gathered to greet them for their appearance on the balcony.

Below right: A smiling Diana waves to the crowd.

Left: Charles and Diana on their honeymoon at Balmoral, following a brief stay at Broadlands, and a two-week cruise around the Mediterranean aboard the Royal Yacht *Britannia*.

Relaxing After the Wedding

Below left: After all the stress and emotion of the wedding, the Royal Family left Heathrow Airport for their annual holiday at Balmoral.

Opposite above: During their break, the Royal Family made the customary trip to the Braemar Highland Games, in what was the first official appearance of the Prince and Princess of Wales after their wedding.

Right: The Queen lent her continued support to the Royal British Legion when she opened its new, modernized headquarters in Pall Mall in November 1981.

Opposite below: Two days later the Queen was in Birmingham on her 34th wedding anniversary. She enjoyed a joke with schoolgirls while on walkabout in Chamberlain Square.

Below right: The Queen and Princess Anne on their way to Horse Guards Parade in May 1982.

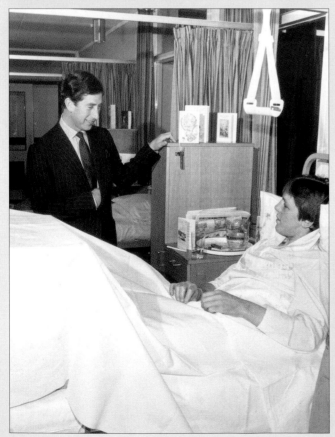

Official Engagements

Opposite above left: In 1982 the Commonwealth Games were held in Brisbane, Australia. Here the Queen hands the baton to England's Brendan Foster.

Opposite above right: The Queen snaps a picture of the closing ceremony of the Commonweath Games in Brisbane.

Opposite below left: Prince Charles meets Mark Davies who was injured during the attack on the *Sir Galahad* during the Falklands War.

Opposite below right: In 1982 the Queen visited the most famous street in Britain when she and Prince Philip inspected the newly-built outdoor location for the long running television program, *Coronation Street*.

Left: Princess Anne mimes drinking to her father at Epsom races in 1982.

Below: The Queen and Prince Philip entertained President Reagan and his wife at Windsor in 1982.

Birth of Prince William

Right: On June 21, 1982 Princess Diana gave birth to a son, William Arthur Philip Louis, who became second in line to the throne. He was born at 9.03pm after a long, sixteen-hour labor and weighed 7lb 1oz. The Queen ordered a forty-one-gun salute at Hyde Park and at the Tower of London.

Above and opposite above: William was christened on August 4 in the Music Room at Buckingham Palace. The Archbishop of Canterbury led the ceremony and the Prince was baptized using water from the River Jordan, a Royal tradition dating back to the time of the Crusades.

Opposite below: In November, just months after the birth, Charles and Diana visited Wales, where they are pictured in Aberdovey.

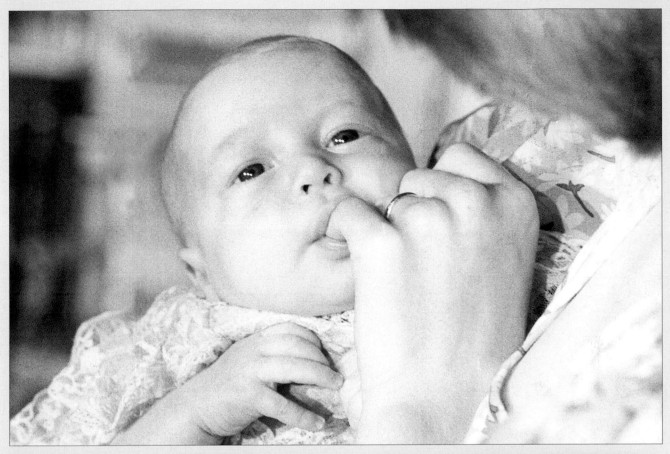

1983: Official Engagements

Opposite above left and right: In June 1983 the Queen opened the new gardens at Croydon Town Hall, marking the centenary of the town's municipal charter.

Right: Several months earlier, in March 1983, the Queen and her grandson, Peter Phillips were forced to walk because they could not find their driver after watching Prince Philip in a carriage driving event at the Royal Windsor Horse Show.

Below right: The Queen presents the Cup after polo at Windsor.

Below: The Queen Mother embraces her grandson Andrew in Scotland after he landed from the Royal Yacht *Britannia*, sporting a beard.

Opposite below left and right: The Royal Family had lunch at Clarence House to mark the Queen Mother's 83rd birthday in August 1983.

Birth of Prince Harry

Left and below left: The following year, on September 15, 1984, two years after the arrival of Prince William, the Princess gave birth to her second son, Prince Henry Charles Albert David.

Below: Hordes of photographers and well-wishers waited outside the hospital for the Princess to emerge with her newborn son.

Opposite below left and right: Earlier in the year the Queen and Prince Philip attended the Annual Stallion Show at Newmarket.

Opposite above: In June 1984 the Queen hosted a special banquet for heads of state at Buckingham Palace, following the London Economic Summit. Margaret Thatcher and Ronald Reagan (shown here to the right of the Queen) were among the guests.

Princess Anne's Young Family

Opposite below right: Zara Phillips at horse trials at Badminton where she was introduced to a Whitbread Shire Horse.

Opposite above: Breaking away from the horse trials, Zara and Peter Phillips enjoyed a freer rein and ran around the grounds with a friend.

Above and below right: Princess Anne walks the dog with her children while taking a break from the Tetbury Horse Trial in September 1984.

Below left: While her mother competed in the Tetbury trial, Zara was looked after by her father Captain Phillips. Princess Michael of Kent also competed and Prince Michael accompanied the Captain at playing nanny.

Opposite below left: During another horse display in 1984, the Queen looked after her young granddaughter, while Princess Anne was busy at work.

Horse play

Right and below: Princess Anne with Peter and Zara at the Windsor Horse Trials.

Opposite above left: The Queen Mother and Prince Charles at the London premiere of *A Passage to India* at the Leicester Square Odeon.

Opposite above right: The Queen attends the Windsor Horse Show to support Prince Philip, who was entered in the carriage driving competition.

Opposite below left: On April 21, 1986 Queen Elizabeth celebrated her 60th birthday. The Royal Family gathered at St. George's Chapel in Windsor to mark the occasion.

Opposite below right: The Queen waves goodbye to the President of Mexico and his wife who had just concluded a state visit in June 1985.

The Duke and Duchess of York

Opposite above: At the beginning of 1986 speculation about a possible Royal engagement was mounting and soon photographers were pursuing Sarah Ferguson. Here she is snapped leaving her house in Clapham the morning before the engagement is made public.

Opposite below: Prince Andrew and Sarah Ferguson announced their engagement on March 19, 1986 with a summer wedding planned. They had met at a dinner party the previous year.

Above: Four months later, on July 23, 1986, they married at Westminster Abbey in a glittering ceremony conducted by the Archbishop of Canterbury, Dr. Robert Runcie. Prince Edward acted as best man. Ninety minutes before the service the Queen conferred the title "Duke of York" on Prince Andrew, a title traditionally reserved for the sovereign's second son.

Left: The newlyweds were at Ascot later in the year.

A Royal Passion for Horses

Right: The Duchess of York and Zara Phillips (now aged 6) pictured with the Queen at the Windsor Horse Show in May 1987. Tim Laurence, who was to eventually marry Princess Anne, can be seen seated behind. He was an Equerry to the Queen when they first met.

Below: The Queen Mother, the Duke of Edinburgh, and Prince Edward were among the congregation that attended a service at Hillington Parish Church near Sandringham.

Opposite above: The Duke and Duchess of York with the Queen at the Royal Horse Trials.

Opposite below: Delighted family members congratulate Princess Anne after she wins the Dresdon Diamond Stakes at Ascot races.

Celebrations

Above: (Left to right) Prince Edward, the Prince and Princess of Wales, the Queen, Viscount Linley, and Lady Sarah Armstrong-Jones join the Queen Mother to celebrate her 87th birthday. Here she greets well-wishers outside the gates of Clarence House.

Left: Lord Snowdon accompanied by his second wife Lucy and son Viscount Linley, attend a society wedding.

Opposite above: Members of the family were present for Amanda Knatchbull's marriage to London property developer Charles Ellingworth at St. Mary's Parish Church in Ashford, Kent.

Opposite below: The Queen greets young well-wishers on a traditional walkabout.

Baby Beatrice

Opposite above and below left: A radiant Duchess of York and a beaming Duke introduced their first baby daughter to the world. Beatrice was born on August 8, 1988 at the Portland Hospital in London.

Opposite below right: While the Duke and Duchess were away in Canada, nanny Olga Powell took Beatrice for a stroll around Windsor Great Park.

Right: Earlier in the year the Queen and Prince Philip attended the Maundy Service at Lichfield Cathedral. During the service she distributed the Royal Maundy Money to sixty-two men and sixty-two women, all aged over 65 years and from the Diocese of Lichfield.

Below right: Here Her Majesty is pictured with the Right Reverend Keith Sutton, Lord Bishop of Lichfield.

Below left: The Queen planting the "Chelsea Sentinel" in the grounds of the Royal Hospital, Chelsea.

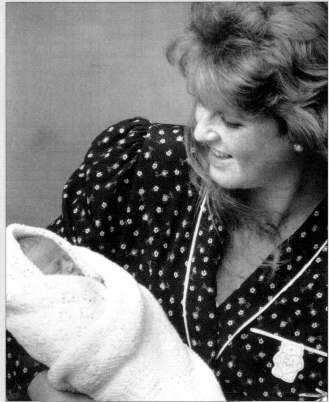

Trooping the Color

Opposite above: Members of the family were on the balcony to watch the Queen's birthday parade after the Trooping the Color ceremony in June 1988. (Left to right) Prince William, Princess of Wales holding Prince Harry, Lady Rose Windsor, Princess Michael cuddling Lady Gabriella Windsor, and Prince Michael of Kent.

Above: Twelve months on and Prince William and Prince Harry were captivated as they watched the 11-plane flypast during the ceremony in 1989. It was the first time Prince Harry had taken part in the carriage procession.

Opposite below: Princess Diana was an incredibly active and popular member of the Royal Family. Here she greets the crowds as she visits St. Catherine's Hospice in Crawley, Surrey.

Left: The Queen and Prince Philip opened a conference at Westminster Hall.

Balmoral Estate

Above: The Queen surveys the Balmoral Estate whilst out riding. She had spent a great deal of time making Balmoral a viable commercial business.

Opposite above: The Queen's Equerry Tim Laurence and a pregnant Duchess of York are with Her Majesty at the Windsor Horse Show in 1989.

Opposite below left: Princess Anne accompanied her mother to the *Joy to the World* Concert at the Royal Albert Hall to mark the 70th anniversary of the Save the Children Fund. The Princess Royal has been President of this charity since 1970.

Opposite below right: Princess Diana arrives at the Canon Cinema, Shaftesbury Avenue for the premiere of *LA Story*.

Left: Another chance for the Queen to visit the Channel Islands as she walks around the Island of Sark.

William's School Days

Right: William began his final year at Wetherby School by attending the Harvest Festival at St. Matthew's Church, Bayswater.

Far right: He was soon playing soccer for Wetherby School and was selected for their first match of the season against Bassett House of Kensington.

Below left: William's final Sports Day at Wetherby ended in tears, after he was disciplined by his mother for disobeying her.

Opposite left: William was met by headmaster Gerald Barber as he began his first day at boarding school in September 1990, attending Ludgrove Preparatory School in Berkshire.

Below right: The Duke and Duchess of York arriving at Heathrow Airport with Beatrice and new baby Eugenie (born on March 23, 1990) after flying back from Buenos Aires. They had been to Argentina to visit the Duchess's step-father Hector Barrantes who had cancer.

Viscount Linley

Top: A smiling Serena Stanhope strolled through Holland Park with a friend, just before her engagement to Viscount Linley was announced.

Above: Viscount Linley and his cousin Lord Lichfield at the party they hosted for 100 friends to celebrate the opening of their second restaurant, situated in Carnaby Street, London.

Royal Life

Opposite above left: The Duchess of York flew back to Heathrow with her daughter Beatrice after a two-day trip to Disneyland with Pamela Stephenson and her three daughters. The following day Beatrice was due to start at Upton House School in Windsor.

Opposite above right: The Queen hands the trophy over to Australia at the Rugby Union World Cup in 1991.

Opposite below: Diana was introduced to Elton John at the Aldwych Theatre, where she attended a fundraising performance of *Tango Argentino*. The money collected was donated to the National Aids Trust.

Above left: Prince Michael of Kent announced that he intended to raise £1 million to build a permanent memorial to his aunt, the Queen Mother, who would soon be celebrating her 91st birthday.

Above right: Continuing with her charity work, Diana attended a dinner at the Mansion House to mark the launch of the Re Action Trust, a charitable venture between industry and Help the Aged.

Left: Members of the family leave church after the service on Christmas morning. Later that day in her speech to the nation, the Queen made it clear that she had no intention of abdicating, ending the speculation that she might step down on the 40th anniversary of her accession.

Beatrice and Eugenie

Opposite left: The Duchess of York leaves Upton House with her younger daughter Eugenie.

Opposite above right: Princess Beatrice was one of the bridesmaids at Annabella Palumbo's wedding.

Opposite below right: Three-year old Beatrice has a right royal tantrum.

Above: The Duke of Edinburgh salutes over a thousand servicemen and women who had served in the Gulf War. Crowds cheered as members of the armed forces marched through the City of London, with the Royal Family taking the official salute from the Mansion House.

Left: The Queen browses through a stall at the Royal Windsor Horse Show in May 1991.

Princess Royal Remarries

Above left: Princess Anne left Heathrow Airport destined for Scotland where she was to marry Commander Timothy Laurence, former Equerry to the Queen, at Craithie Church near Balmoral.

Above right: The wedding took place on December 12, 1992 with the couple determined to keep it a very private occasion. After the service the newlyweds drove away in their Range Rover.

Right: Another member of the Royal Family to marry that year was Lady Helen Windsor. Her wedding to art dealer Tim Taylor took place at St. George's Chapel, Windsor.

Opposite above: Members of the Royal Family turned out for the wedding in force. Prince Charles and Prince Andrew lead, followed by Princess Anne and Prince Edward, with Diana behind in a vivid green outfit.

Opposite below left: Sarah, Duchess of York keeps a tight hand on Beatrice and Eugenie.

Opposite below right: William finding his feet on a skiing trip to Austria.

Family Occasions

Above left and right: Thorpe Park proved a firm favorite with Princes William and Harry, who enjoyed a day there with their mother in 1993.

Right: The young princes with their great-grandmother.

Opposite above: The Queen points a stern finger as she enjoys a day at Epsom races with her mother and son.

Opposite below left: The Duke of Edinburgh with his three sons and grandson Peter Phillips, were among the members of the family who attended a Carol Service at the church near Sandringham.

Opposite below right: The Queen Mother at the Remembrance Service in Westminster Abbey, 1993.

93rd Birthday

Opposite above: The family gather at Clarence House for the Queen Mother's 93rd birthday.

Opposite below left: Later that evening the Queen Mother was at the Prince Edward Theatre with her daughter to see *Crazy for You*.

Opposite below right: Later in the year at Bisley in Surrey, the Queen was given the opportunity to fire the last shot of the Centenary event using an SA80 rifle.

Right: A chance for the Queen to go shopping at Windsor Horse Show.

Below: Princess Diana makes a visit to the Royal Hospital to meet the Chelsea pensioners.

The Young Princes

Opposite above: William arrives at Wimbledon to watch the women's final.

Opposite below left: William with his father.

Opposite below right: Harry happily leaves a store with his mother.

Below left and right: The Princes leave the Chicago Rib Shack in Knightsbridge, London in January 1995.

Left: Already an accomplished rider, Harry took part in the Beaufort Hunt when he was eleven.

William at Eton

Left and below: William arriving to begin his schooling at Eton in September 1995. Although by now his parents were in the process of divorcing, the family arrived together.

Opposite below right: William achieved both academic and sporting success at Eton. He gained nine GCSE and three A level certificates. He was a very good swimmer, a fearless soccer player and was soon in the school team.

Opposite above left: A St. Patrick's Day visit for the Queen Mother to the Irish Guards Barracks in Chelsea for the annual distribution of shamrocks.

Opposite above center: The Queen enjoying the Windsor Horse Show in 1995.

Opposite above right: An eager grandmother arrives at the home of Daniel and Lady Sarah Chatto who were awaiting the birth of their first child.

Opposite below left: The Queen and Queen Mother watch the 50th anniversary of the Victory in Europe celebrations in London from the balcony of Buckingham Palace.

A Son for Lady Sarah

Opposite above: Lady Sarah Chatto and her husband Daniel leave the Portland Hospital in London with their four-day-old son. He was later named Samuel David Benedict Chatto.

Opposite below left and right: Earlier in the year the Queen chose to celebrate her 70th birthday with minimum fuss. After attending a church service at Sandringham with Princess Anne, she spent time afterwards talking to children, many of whom presented her with flowers.

Left: Camilla Parker-Bowles with her son Tom and daughter Laura, at Henry Dent-Brocklehurst's 30th birthday party at the Cafe Royal. She was later seen chatting to her ex-husband Andrew and his new wife Rosemary.

Below right: On arrival in Fredericton, Canada, Prince Charles' first duty was to inspect the honor guard mounted by the 2nd Battalion, Royal Canadian Regiment.

Below left: Prince William and Peter and Zara Phillips share a joke as they leave church after the Christmas Day service at Sandringham.

William and Harry

Below: Harry, seen here on vacation at Klosters. After many skiing trips he had become a very confident and able skier.

Right: The family were united for Prince William's confirmation at St. George's Chapel in Windsor in March 1997. It was the first time Charles and Diana had appeared together in public since their divorce the previous August.

Opposite above: The boys at Polvier by the River Dee in Scotland with their father. It was near the end of this summer vacation that they would hear the tragic news of their mother's death.

Opposite below: On a visit to Duku Duku in South Africa, Charles and Harry took time out to watch some Zulu dancing.

The Death of the Princess

Above: On August 31, 1997, Princess Diana was tragically killed in a high-speed car crash in Paris. The Princes, who were with their father at Balmoral at the time, were informed the following morning. Immediately the announcement was made public, a massive outpouring of grief seemed to sweep the nation, with floral tributes swamping the entrance to Kensington Palace.

Left: Prince Charles attempts to console his distraught sons.

Opposite above: Diana's funeral took place at Westminster Abbey on September 6. One million people were estimated to have lined the procession route.

Opposite below: Charles, Prince Philip, the young Princes, and Earl Spencer, Diana's brother, stand in silence as the coffin is carried past them into the Abbey.

Clarence House

Opposite above: The family gathers at Clarence House to celebrate the Queen Mother's 98th birthday.

Opposite below: Prince William and Zara Phillips share a secret during the celebrations.

Below left: A reflective Zara Phillips at her great-grandmother's birthday.

Below right: The Queen Mother and Princess Margaret share a carriage for the Trooping the Color ceremony in 1998.

Left: Later in the year the Queen, with a very somber face, is seen here at St. Mary's Cathedral, Kuala Lumpar. She had just learned of the death of Susan Barrantes, mother of the Duchess of York.

Edward and Sophie

The Queen's youngest child, Prince Edward, married Sophie Rhys-Jones at Windsor in June, an occasion that was noted for its comparatively informal atmosphere. Afterwards, Edward was given the title Earl of Wessex and Sophie became H.R.H. the Countess of Wessex.

Opposite above left and right: As the engagement was announced in London on January 6, 1999, the couple posed for photographs and walked in the garden of St. James's Palace. They stated that they were hoping for a late spring wedding in St. George's Chapel in Windsor.

Right: Edward and his future wife Sophie talking as they watched the Queen's birthday salute (Trooping the Color) on the balcony at Buckingham Palace, a week before their wedding.

Below and opposite below: The couple married on June 19, 1999, and after the ceremony traveled back to the reception at Windsor Castle in a landau, waving to the crowds as they did so.

Riding and Skiing

Opposite above: Princess Anne and her daughter, Zara Phillips, riding in the grounds of Windsor Castle.

Opposite below: The Princes joking with their father following William's first driving lesson at Highgrove in July 1999. His lesson had been given by police driving instructor Sergeant Chris Gilbert.

Above and left: Princes William and Harry developed a closer relationship with their father in the years following the death of Princess Diana. Here they enjoyed a skiing trip together at Klosters in Switzerland.

A Landmark Anniversary

A host of notable Royal birthdays took place in 2000—Princess Margaret celebrated her 70th, the Princess Royal her 50th, Prince William came of age and the Duke of York was 40. But it was the Queen Mother's 100th birthday that stood out as the landmark anniversary, and her whole family helped her celebrate.

Opposite above right: In July, the Royal Family attended a Thanksgiving Service at St Paul's Cathedral to celebrate the Queen Mother's life. The Princess Royal, the Earl and Countess of Wessex, Prince Andrew, Peter Phillips, and Princesses Beatrice and Eugenie are seen standing on the steps after the service.

Right: Princesses Eugenie and Beatrice waved to the crowds as they left St. Paul's after the Thanksgiving Service.

Below: Members of the Royal Family joined the Queen Mother on the balcony of Buckingham Palace on her 100th birthday, August 4, 2000.

Opposite above left: Princess Beatrice with her father, the Duke of York, after they and the rest of the Royal Family attended a Sunday service at St. Mary Magdalene Church in Sandringham, Norfolk.

A Year of Anxiety

The outbreak of foot and mouth disease in Britain in February 2001 caused anxiety for many, but it was the terrorist attacks on New York on September 11, that were to be the defining moment of the year.

Opposite above: The Queen Mother walked out of Clarence House with the aid of her walking sticks to greet the crowds on her 101st birthday. Accompanying her are (front row L–R): Princess Beatrice, Queen Elizabeth II, Princess Eugenie, and the Duke of York. (back row L–R): the Duke of Edinburgh, Prince Harry, Prince Charles, Prince William, Zara Phillips, Peter Phillips, the Princess Royal, Lady Sarah Chatto, and Commander Tim Laurence.

Opposite below: Prince William and Prince Harry after the Sandringham Service.

Above: Prince Harry with his cousin, Zara Phillips, at the Christmas Sandringham Service.

Left: Prince Harry at the Six Nations Rugby Tournament, watching England beat Wales 50–10.

A Year of Sadness and Celebration

The Queen's Golden Jubilee celebrations, to mark 50 years as monarch, were set to dominate the Royal year, but this was not to be. After suffering heart problems following a stroke, the Queen's sister, Princess Margaret, died on February 9 at the age of 71. Less than two months later, in her 102nd year, the Queen Mother died peacefully in her sleep at Windsor.

Above center: The Queen arriving at Westminster Abbey for a memorial service for Princess Margaret.

Above left: Princes William and Harry following the gun carriage that carried the Queen Mother's coffin to Westminster Hall for her lying-in-state.

Opposite below: The Queen Mother lay-in-state for five days in Westminster Hall, where mourners filed past the coffin to pay their respects.

Opposite above: The Earl and Countess of Wessex viewing the flowers left by members of the public for the Queen Mother.

Above right: The funeral took place on April 9 at Westminster Abbey. Here Prince Charles, visibly moved, watches the coffin leaving the Abbey.

Left: The Queen out riding in the grounds of Windsor Castle.

Golden Jubilee

Opposite above left: In June 2002 Queen Elizabeth II celebrated her Golden Jubilee, having reigned as monarch for 50 years. The event was marked by extensive celebrations, including a thanksgiving service at St. Paul's Cathedral, a parade and carnival along The Mall, a flypast involving the Red Arrows and Concorde, the Party at the Palace concert (at Buckingham Palace), and a huge firework display. Here the Queen makes her way to St. Paul's in the Gold State coach, which she had previously used only for her coronation and Silver Jubilee celebrations.

Opposite above right: Edward and Sophie, the Earl and Countess of Wessex, leave Buckingham Palace for St. Paul's in an open-topped coach.

Left: Andrew, the Duke of York, and Princes William and Harry also ride in an open carriage as part of the procession, accompanied by a mounted escort.

Below: The Princes and the Duke of York arriving at St. Paul's.

Opposite below: Prince William, Prince Charles, and the Queen sharing a joke as they observe the spectacular carnival in The Mall.

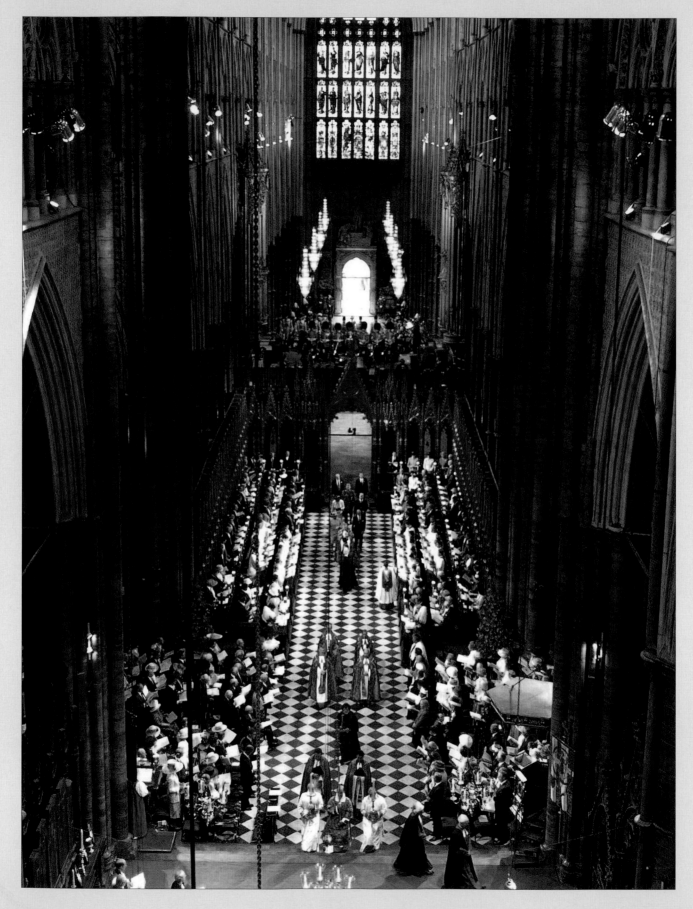

Renewing Her Vows

Another milestone was reached with the 50th anniversary of the Queen's Coronation on June 2, 2003. A service at Westminster Abbey on the day, saw the Queen renewing her vows of 50 years ago.

Opposite: The Queen and the Duke of Edinburgh are led in procession by the Dean of Westminster, the Very Reverend Dr. Wesley Carr, at the start of the service in Westminster Abbey.

Above: The Queen and Prince Philip with their grandsons, Princes William and Harry, on the balcony at the Trooping the Color.

Left: The Queen visiting St. Bartholomew the Great Church in the City of London.

Diana Memorial

After much controversy, the Diana Memorial Fountain was officially opened in Hyde Park during the summer of 2004. But the year ended on a tragic note with the loss of over 200,000 lives in the tsunami which hit large parts of South-East Asia after Christmas.

Opposite below: American President George W. Bush and Mrs Bush met the Queen and Prince Philip at Buckingham Palace on their first state visit to Britain in November 2003.

Opposite above left: Prince Charles with former glider pilots at the Pegasus Bridge Monument in Normandy on the anniversary of D-Day in June 2004.

Opposite above right: In July 2004 Prince Charles visited the site of a more recent conflict, the Old Bridge in Mostar, Bosnia, which had recently been rebuilt.

Left: July 2004 also saw the Party in the Park at Hyde Park, in aid of the Prince's Trust. Prince Charles is pictured with the singer Jamelia who is an ambassador for the organization.

Below: Prince Charles and his sons attended the official unveiling by the Queen of the Diana Memorial Fountain in Hyde Park, London on July 6.

Charles Marries Camilla

More than thirty years after they first met, the Prince of Wales and Camilla Parker Bowles were married in a civil ceremony at Windsor Guildhall on April 9, 2004. This was followed with a blessing by the Archbishop of Canterbury in St. George's Chapel and then a reception for 800 invited guests in the state apartments at Windsor Castle.

Opposite: Guests and spectators arriving for the wedding in Windsor.

Left: Prince Charles and his new bride, now known as the Duchess of Cornwall, left St. George's Chapel after the blessing to a warm reception from the waiting crowds.

Below: The Duchess of Cornwall at St. George's Chapel.

The Prince and Duchess

Below: Prince Harry, Zara Phillips, and Prince William at the wedding of the Princes' father to Camilla Parker Bowles.

Right: Prince William arriving by coach at the Guildhall in Windsor.

Opposite above: The Prince of Wales and the Duchess of Cornwall at St. George's Chapel, Windsor.

Opposite below: Members of the Royal Family gather around the Royal couple after the blessing at St. George's Chapel.

A Family Affair

Opposite: Prince Charles and the Duchess of Cornwall leave the Guildhall after their civil ceremony, followed by Princes William and Harry.

Below: Prince William, Prince Harry, and Peter and Zara Phillips, following the marriage blessing at St. George's Chapel.

Left: Prince Charles, the Duchess of Cornwall, and Prince Harry after the blessing.

William Graduates

Right: In June 2005 Prince William graduated from the University of St. Andrews, having gained a Masters degree in Geography.

Opposite left: The Duchess of Cornwall is pictured with Prince Charles, opening a playground near Balmoral; her first official engagement since they were married.

Below: In the same month, the Prince and the Duchess arrived in the royal carriage for Ladies' Day at the Royal Ascot meeting. The event was held at York because of construction work being undertaken at Ascot Racecourse.

Opposite above right: In October 2005, on a state visit to Lithuania, the Queen and Prince Philip attended a banquet at the Presidential Palace hosted by President Yaldas Adamkus.

Opposite below right: The Queen whilst on a visit in May 2006 to a dairy farm in Clitheroe, Lancashire.

The Queen at 80

The Queen turned 80 on April 21, 2006 and many celebrations and events took place both around this date and on her official birthday on June 17. Services of thanksgiving were held, along with lunches, dinners, firework displays, receptions, and even a children's party at Buckingham Palace.

Left: On the steps of St. Paul's Cathedral after the thanksgiving service for the Queen's 80th birthday. Pictured L-R: the Earl and Countess of Wessex, Prince Charles, Prince Harry, Prince William, Princess Beatrice, and the Duke of York. The Princess Royal and Commander Tim Laurence can be seen in the background.

Below: The Queen and the Duke of Edinburgh in full regalia attending the Order of the Garter Ceremony at Windsor Castle.

The Family Celebrate

To celebrate her 80th birthday, the Queen took her family on a cruise around the Western Isles in July on the cruise ship, *The Hebridean Princess*.

Left: Princess Anne and her husband Tim Laurence board the ship.

Opposite above left: Princesses Beatrice and Eugenie on their way to *The Hebridean Princess*.

Opposite below right: Lady Louise Windsor enjoying the sunshine.

Opposite below left: Lady Sarah Chatto, Daniel Chatto, Viscount and Viscountess Linley, and the Honorable Margarita Armstrong-Jones.

Opposite above right: Prince Charles pictured aboard the cruise liner.

Below: Celebrations continued as the Queen toured Lithuania.

Following pages: Prince William, on parade at Sandhurst in December 2006, struggles to hide his amusement as The Queen, his grandmother, inspects the troops. Much has changed since George V established the House of Windsor in 1917 and members of the Royal Family have had increasingly to adapt to living in the public eye. The Queen, in the 55th year of her remarkable reign, has stood at the head of the Family, working to transform it into a modern monarchy, able to act as a focus for national identity and unity into the 21st century.

Acknowledgments

The photographs in this book are from the archives of the *Daily Mail*.
Particular thanks to Steve Torrington, Alan Pinnock, Katie Lee,
Dave Sheppard, Brian Jackson, Richard Jones, and all the staff.

Design by John Dunne.